Other books by Matthew S. Chan

The Intrepid Way
How to Create the Freedom You Need to Live the Life You Want!

TurnKey Investing with Lease-Options
How to Simply & Safely Create 12% Returns with Investment Property!

The TurnKey Investor's "Subject to" Mortgage Handbook
The Art & Science of Buying Investment Property by Taking Over Mortgages!

Essential Lease-Option Lessons
TurnKey Investing Stories & Case Studies from the Field!

The Intrepid Way II – Transformation
The Journey & Escape from Corporate World to Entrepreneurial Freedom!

www.turnkeyinvesting.com

The TurnKey Investor's

"Subject To" Mortgage Handbook

The Art & Science of Buying Investment Property by Taking Over Mortgages!

Matthew S. Chan

Author of "TurnKey Investing with Lease-Options"

With Contributions by Wes Weaver

Ascend Beyond Publishing
Columbus, Georgia

The TurnKey Investor's "Subject To" Mortgage Handbook
The Art & Science of Buying Investment Property by Taking Over Mortgages!

Published by: Ascend Beyond Publishing
5435 Woodruff Farm Rd., #B-300
PMB 158
Columbus, GA 31907

www.ascendbeyond.com

ISBN: 0-9713947-4-1

Printed in the United States of America. First Edition.

First Printing: August 2005

Book Ordering Information
Visit **www.turnkeyinvesting.com** to order additional copies for private use or for resale. Quantity discounts are available. Special pricing for churches, schools, colleges, universities, and non-profit, charitable organizations.

Visit our website at **www.turnkeyinvesting.com** to find more information on books, educational materials, and courses on how to create safe and steady returns through real estate investments.

Dedication

To the people who have entrusted me ...

To the people who have invested with me ...

To the independent-minded investor ...

To the supporters of TurnKey Investing ...

I commit this book to them. Salute.

Matthew S. Chan

Table of Contents

Introduction

CHAPTER 1 The Beauty of "Subject to" Mortgages

CHAPTER 2 The Fundamentals of "Subject to" Mortgages

CHAPTER 3 Legitimizing "Subject to" Mortgage Transactions

CHAPTER 4 Finding the Urgent Seller

CHAPTER 5 Evaluating Potential Deals

CHAPTER 6 The Risks of "Subject to" Mortgage Transactions

CHAPTER 9 After the Closing

CHAPTER 10 Ongoing Issues

CHAPTER 11 The TurnKey Investing Philosophy

Conclusion

Appendix

Bonus Book Excerpt:

Introduction

In 1999, I decided that I wanted to acquire a "large" portfolio of investment property. Specifically, I wanted to buy single-family houses that produced monthly cash flow. I didn't simply want to "dabble" in real estate like so many people do by only buying 1, 2,or 3 properties. Long-term, I want to buy 10, 20, 30 properties and more.

I knew building this property portfolio was not going to be an overnight venture. It was going to take time and lots of work over the course of several years.

The Dilemma

One of the major obstacles I saw in acquiring the portfolio size I wanted was my limited borrowing power. I knew it would not be difficult to qualify for a few loans through a mortgage broker on my own but I also realized that it would not take long for my credit to get tapped out.

When I began acquiring properties, I was a self-employed, independent contractor in the I.T. industry, not a W-2 wage earner. As you might expect, lenders much prefer a high-paid W-2 wage earner to a self-employed individual. I knew this going in.

I have always taken a proactive approach in any business I am in. I was not comfortable with the idea of being tapped out of financial resources first then trying to find a solution around it.

One rule I follow in business and investing is, "Get money when you don't need it." Conversely, the worst time to look for financing is when you are tapped out and desperately need it. It is a basic law of credit. When you have little or no debt, everyone wants to loan you money and give credit. When you finally do take on lots of debt, lenders pull back on credit and get nervous about lending money.

A Working Solution

Like many beginning investors, I exclusively used my own cash and credit to buy my first few properties to get myself going. But I knew I would have to as quickly as possible find alternative ways to finance properties I wanted to buy.

I read and studied various methods of alternative financing and I realized if I wanted to bypass conventional lenders, I would have to utilize *seller-financing*. One seller-financing technique I learned, adapted, and used, is the *"subject to" mortgage* where we "take over" mortgages on an existing property. I refer to this form of seller-financing as an equivalent to "assuming a non-assumable loan."

I must admit that while I initially understood the concept, I was a bit slow and clumsy in execution. The reason why I was slow and clumsy is so much of the success of using this technique is based on the ability to negotiate, educate, and create trust with the sellers.

The Start

I had a slow start in 1999 as I was simultaneously trying to buy property but having to travel frequently in my I.T. training business. By early 2000, I managed to acquire a few investment properties in the Atlanta area when I decided that I both wanted and needed to relocate to a smaller city. The city I eventually relocated to was Columbus, Georgia, two hours southwest of Atlanta next to the Alabama border.

The Alliance

In early 2001, I settled in and got established enough in my new home city of Columbus to begin resuming property acquisitions. By the end of 2001, I would go on to acquire five more investment properties with "subject to" mortgage financing. It was during this time I met my current business partner, Wes Weaver (also the Lead Contributor of this book).

Wes watched with great interest how I, one by one, negotiated and executed "subject to" mortgages to acquire investment property and then created cash flow by lease-optioning them out.

Starting out as my apprentice, Wes eventually joined forces with me to create a management alliance we enjoy today. Together, we have gone on to become the *"#1 Provider of Owner-Financed Homes in Columbus, Georgia & Phenix City, Alabama"* where we specialize in lease-optioning property out to our tenant-buyers.

How we lease-option out properties we acquire is covered in the previous book, *"TurnKey Investing with Lease-Options"*.

The How-to Manual

This book discusses how Wes and I jointly acquire investment properties with "subject to" mortgages. Wes and I take a unique tag-team and synergistic approach in our "subject to" mortgage transactions. Together, we carry more credibility and close more transactions than if we did them separately.

At the risk of being boastful, the book you have in your hands contains an incredible amount of little-known information never before seen in book format. And while there are other sources of "subject to" mortgage information which you can learn from, very few contain the in-depth research and the customized techniques described herein. I am confident that you will find distinctions not found elsewhere.

The Reasons for Writing this Book

This book was written for several reasons:

First, because we value our business reputation, we always look to maintain a high degree of credibility and legitimacy in what we do. "Subject to" mortgage transactions are often unknown or misunderstood. This manual serves as a definitive written source explaining how and why we do what we do.

Second, because we invite investment partners to work with us, this book allows us to more completely and efficiently describe and communicate what we do without all the fluff of a brochure.

Third, as our management team grows, this book serves as both an instructional and operational guide into what and how we do things. It is a more concise alternative to a full-scale Operations Manual.

Finally, this book was written for experienced investors who wish to expand their financial repertoire by utilizing the "subject to" mortgage as an additional financing technique to acquire property.

What to Keep in Mind

There are two important points I want you to keep in mind.

Despite how the "subject to" mortgage technique is advertised in seminar circles, we take a serious view on this subject. We consider this an advanced financing technique that can be incredibly powerful when utilized correctly. Or it can be financially catastrophic in foolish or ignorant hands. *This handbook was written for the experienced investor* and makes no effort to accommodate the beginning investor.

Our system constantly changes and evolves as we adapt to new circumstances, situations, rules, and market conditions. As such, we unhesitatingly make changes, updates, and revisions to our daily operations which, over the course of time, may outdate the information in this book.

In the meantime, I hope you find the information helpful. Thank you for reading this book.

Matthew S. Chan

CHAPTER

1

The Beauty of "Subject to" Mortgages

The idea of buying investment property without having to get a new loan is a very attractive idea. One way this occurs is that you take title to a property but leave your seller's existing loan in place. This particular method of acquiring property is the essence of a little-known technique of buying and financing property with a *"subject to" mortgage*, a form of seller-financing.

The Benefits

There are many benefits to buying property with the "subject to" mortgage technique, including:

- No Qualification Process
- Fast Closings
- No Loan Costs
- No Impact on Borrowing Power
- Negative Events Do Not Appear on Our Credit Report
- Profitably Buy Little or "No Equity" Properties
- Seller's Credit is Often Improved
- Lender Losses are Minimized

No Qualification Process

When we buy property with a "subject to" mortgage, we are not "asking permission" from a lender as to whether we can buy the property and qualify for a loan. Neither are we trying to formally "assume" the loan.

We are simply making alternative offers to sellers (who already went through a loan qualification process) for us to step in, take over their position, and begin making payments. In effect, we bypass the normally cumbersome loan qualification process.

Fast Closings

Because we are simply assuming the seller's position with the loan, we are able to do quick closings. Often, all that is required for a closing on such properties is for us to do a title check, verify the loan status with the lender, and then set up an appointment with a real estate attorney (or title company) to complete the paperwork and close the deal. Typically, all these events can happen within a week.

We use this benefit in our negotiations with our sellers who may want to move out and on with their lives quickly.

No Loan Costs

Buying investment property typically requires getting new financing, which often means qualifying for a new loan. When a lender agrees to provide financing to a borrower, theses loans and closing costs can add several thousand dollars to the purchase price of the property. Such costs can include fees for appraisals, loan underwriting, attorneys, couriers, surveys, insurance, and inspections. The list of the fees to be paid for a new loan can be quite long.

Buying property with a "subject to" mortgage eliminates the loan fees and closing costs because they were already paid by the seller when they originally bought the property. The only exception to this no-fee approach is that when we close with our sellers, we pay our real estate attorney a fee to do our closings.

No Impact on Borrowing Power

A common challenge for many real estate investors is the amount of financing they can qualify for as their portfolio grows. With every new investment loan, an investor's borrowing power generally weakens. Ultimately, many investors will encounter a time when getting new investment properties with their own borrowing power becomes very difficult.

Buying properties with a "subject to" mortgage bypasses any impact on our credit reports and our borrowing power. The reason is that the loan continues to appear on the seller's credit report until we ultimately pay off and satisfy the loan. As such, there is not a credit limit to how many properties we can buy with a "subject to" mortgage.

"Ultimately, many investors will encounter a time when getting new investment properties with their own borrowing power becomes very difficult."

Negative Events Do Not Appear on Our Credit Report

I almost hesitate to bring this benefit up because this can be taken out of context, but I will do so in the interest of being complete. It is a benefit I hope no one -- including ourselves -- **ever** takes advantage of.

In the highly improbable event that we lost a property to foreclosure, our credit reports would not show any negative consequences. To a lesser degree, even late payments and other negative performance-related issues will not appear on our credit reports. If a foreclosure occurs, it will appear on the seller's credit report.

> *"Buying properties with a 'subject to' mortgage bypasses any impact on our credit reports and our borrowing power."*

At this point, I would like to emphatically point out that this benefit can only be used under financially or economically catastrophic events. Like life insurance, this is a benefit you hope to never use in your lifetime.

I do not in any way, shape, or form condone buying a property with a "subject to" mortgage if there is any question or concern about whether you can make the payments. This is especially true if you are buying from a seller who has marginal to excellent credit. Buying properties with a "subject to" mortgage is just as serious a business, if not more so, as buying property with your own credit. If you ruin your own credit, that is one thing – but ruining another person's credit is a burden being placed on someone else.

Yet if an economic catastrophe occurs, you can take some small comfort that your credit will not be ruined by the properties you bought with a "subject to" mortgage.

Profitably Buy Little or "No Equity" Properties

One of our favorite ways to separate ourselves from many buyers in our market is that we are able to profitably buy little or "no equity" properties. Typically, sellers with no equity in their property have a difficult time selling them. In our local area, it is quite common for many sellers who have owned their homes for three years or less to have little or no equity in their property. Clearly, we are nowhere near California cities or any of the other places where property appreciates very quickly.

> *"If an economic catastrophe occurs, you can take some small comfort that your credit will not likely be ruined by the properties you bought with a 'subject to' mortgage."*

When a seller wants to mortgage a property with little or no equity, very few real estate agents are willing to work with sellers of those properties because their sales commissions often come from the proceeds of a sale. If there is little or no equity, the only way a real estate agent could be paid is if a seller is willing to pay the commission out of pocket. Needless to say, few sellers are inclined or are prepared to pay such a large sales commission themselves.

As investors buying for profit, we would not normally get new financing to buy little or no equity properties. Because a new loan would add thousands of dollars to the purchase price (making it over-priced), it would make little sense to go through the trouble or costs to buy these types of properties.

However, buying with a "subject to" mortgage increases our willingness and the overall desirability of the property because it allows us to step into those properties with great ease, little out of pocket costs, and no loan qualification process.

Seller's Credit is Often Improved

Often, we buy from sellers with a troubled payment record. They frequently have loan arrearages they cannot pay. In some situations, foreclosure is imminent. When we step in to buy these properties, we pay the arrearage and reinstate the loan.

Once we reinstate the loan, we begin to make regular monthly payments to the seller's account. From the lender's point of view, the account has "miraculously" improved. From the seller's point of view, their troubled credit "magically" begins improving as their delinquent account and arrearage disappears and the account becomes and stays current. Over a 12-month period, having a mortgage loan that is current goes a long way to improving the seller's credit score and borrowing power.

> *"Often, we buy from sellers with a troubled payment record."*

And as part of our negotiations, we often tell our sellers about this particular benefit. Not only do they sell their property quickly but also they get their credit scores and credit records improved because of it.

Lender Losses are Minimized

Lenders are helped by "subject to" mortgage transactions. By creatively utilizing this technique, we often save properties and loans from foreclosure action.

Foreclosure action is generally a very expensive process where many parties lose. The borrower would clearly vacate the property and suffer a foreclosure record. But the lender often takes business losses by paying fees on foreclosing and managing vacant properties that have little or no equity.

Additionally, when they do finally resell the properties, they often do not fully recover the monies they originally loaned out. These costs are passed on to future loan customers.

> *"We often save properties and loans from foreclosure action."*

By doing our part to "save" the properties and the accompanying loans, lenders suffer fewer losses from foreclosure action. More importantly, they continue to have a performing account with ongoing loan payments.

Summary

Buying and financing investment properties with a "subject to" mortgage has many benefits for the buyer, the seller, and the lender. A "subject to" mortgage is not a "magical pill" to solve all buyer, seller, or lender problems. However, it is an innovative and little-known financing technique that, when properly utilized, provides win-win situations to all parties.

CHAPTER

2

The Fundamentals of "Subject to" Mortgages

There are various elements and concepts that you must understand in order to digest the mechanics of an entire "subject to" mortgage transaction.

Conceptually speaking, buying property with a "subject to" mortgage involves transferring title from a seller to a buyer while preserving the integrity and terms of the existing loan. In essence, you are buying the property "subject to" the terms of the existing loan.

The title changes hands, but the original loan stays in place. The original borrower retains formal liability on the loan. When this occurs, the seller has provided the buyer a form of "seller-financing" to make the deal happen.

There are several components and surrounding issues that you have to first understand before you engage in a "subject to" mortgage transaction.

Assuming a "Non-Assumable" Loan

The nature of a "subject to" mortgage is that we are in essence assuming a "non-assumable" loan. We do so without going through any qualification process, and the transaction is done without direct permission from the lender.

Components of a "Subject to" Mortgage Transaction

The major components of a "subject to" mortgage transaction are:

- Title
- Legal Possession
- Lender
- Loan
- Mortgage
- Seller / Borrower
- Buyer

Title

Every property has a legal entity that owns, controls, or holds the title to that property. That legal entity could be a corporation, partnership, trust, or individual. Having title is what gives you the right to control or own a property.

That title can be conveyed from one legal entity to another. Title is transferred and conveyed most often by a document called a Warranty Deed.

The essence of transferring title from one party to another involves the following steps.

- A new Warranty Deed is prepared (often by a real estate attorney).

Mechanics of "Subject to" Mortgage Transaction

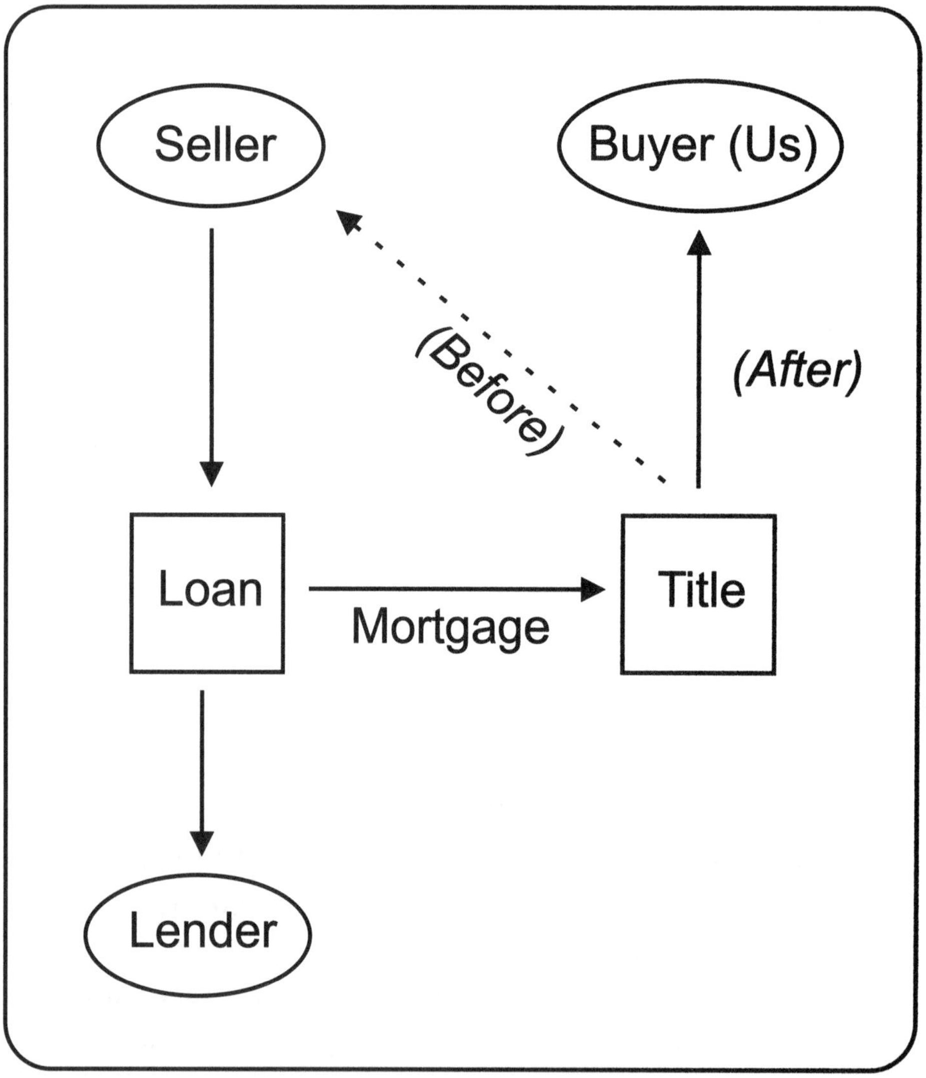

- The legal owner/title holder signs that Warranty Deed to another party (most often a Buyer).
- The new Warranty Deed is recorded at the courthouse.

Simplistically speaking, those are the essential steps of transferring title.

Legal Possession

You can have title to a property but not have legal possession of the property. This most commonly occurs when dealing with rental property. For example, a landlord investor typically holds title to a rental property. However, by agreeing to lease that property to a tenant, the landlord investor gives legal possession (occupancy and usage rights) to the tenant.

> *"You can have title to a property but not have legal possession of the property."*

The only way that landlord investor could get legal possession back is if the tenant voluntarily exits the lease and gave the keys back. The other way is through an eviction process – but only with due and justifiable cause such as non-payment and other significant breaches of the lease.

In a "subject to" mortgage transaction, I caution people to get both title and legal possession of the property as quickly as possible. Taking title without quickly getting legal possession (from the original owner or from an existing tenant) is generally not a good idea.

Lender

The lender is the bank or finance company that provides funds to borrowers to buy property. The lender sets the qualifications a borrower must meet to get a loan. The lender also sets up the terms and conditions by which the borrower agrees to and must repay the loan. Those terms include, but are not limited to, the amount borrowed, the down payment, loan costs, payment schedule, interest rate, and total interest paid.

In this book, we will refer to any entity holding and servicing a loan as the lender. That party may not have been the original lender. However, when the original lender transfers and assigns a loan to another company, the company to which the loan is assigned becomes, in effect, the new lender.

Loan

A borrower has to qualify for a loan, thereby incurring a debt to buy a house. A promissory note often details the specific terms of loan repayment such as interest rate, term of the loan, and the monthly payment.

The loan is often maintained and serviced by a lender or servicing agency. Loans are frequently sold and transferred to other lenders or servicing agencies to maintain. Borrowers continue to make payments to the new lender or servicing agency under the same terms set by the original lender.

> *"A mortgage is often confused with the loan used to purchase a property."*

Mortgage

A mortgage is often confused with the loan used to purchase a property.

Technically, a mortgage is a separate legal instrument that lenders use to place a lien upon a property to formally secure the loan they made to a borrower.

As such, when a buyer uses money from a lender to buy a property, the buyer becomes the mortgagor. People who buy real property with borrowed money are typically mortgagors.

The lender is typically the mortgagee who holds a lien upon a property.

If a mortgage did not exist to secure a loan to a given property, lenders would not be protected if their payers stopped paying. The mortgage makes provisions for lenders to protect their financial interests by having the ability to foreclose on properties with loans in severe default.

Because so many people use the word "mortgage" to mean the "secured loan" of a property, I will take artistic license to use that term interchangeably with the word "loan" for the sake of easy readability and convenience. For this one chapter, the terms "loan" and "mortgage" will have two distinct meanings.

Seller / Borrower

In the context of this book, our sellers are also the original borrowers of the loans we take over. In effect, our sellers sell their property to us under the conditions of their original loan.

We will use the term "seller" and "borrower" interchangeably to denote the same person.

Buyer

We often refer to ourselves as the Buyer. As buyers, we assume the role of investors who buy property for investment purposes, not for personal residential usage.

As investor-buyers in a "subject to" mortgage transaction, we have a responsibility to make intelligent decisions to ensure every party's interests are protected. However, we also have a responsibility to profit from every investment to ensure the viability of the portfolio we maintain and pay on.

Legitimizing "Subject to" Mortgage Transactions

"Subject to" mortgages are easily misunderstood and often cause distress and confusion to the uninformed. How you position the transaction, educate the people you work with, and ultimately execute the "subject to" mortgage transaction will in the long term determine your success with this particular technique.

Later in this book, I address the potential skepticism and credibility issues surrounding doing "subject to" mortgage transactions.

Additionally, I have assembled a list of credible written works in the area of "subject to" mortgage transactions which provide hard-core support against the arguments that even the most pessimistic skeptic may raise.

This subject is more thoroughly covered in Chapter 3.

Urgent Sellers

While there are many technical issues regarding "subject to" mortgage transactions, the success of making it work comes down to the human element of finding a receptive and agreeable seller. The most elegant transactions can only occur with the cooperation of a willing and trusting seller who has a sense of need and urgency.

> *"Skeptics tend to believe deception, coercion, or desperation is required to do such a deal."*

We frequently encounter uninformed people who cannot fathom the rationale that makes a seller agreeable to a "subject to" mortgage transaction. Skeptics and cynics tend to believe deception, coercion, or desperation is required to do each and every deal. As the old saying goes, nothing is further from the truth.

Many of the questions such as "How could anyone agree to do a 'subject to' mortgage transaction?" or "Why would anyone do such a deal?" are answered in this book.

This subject is more thoroughly covered in Chapter 4.

Evaluating Potential Deals

Once a potential seller is agreeable to the idea of a "subject to" mortgage transaction, what happens next? We have to evaluate the deal. Checking the lender, the status of the loan, the profit potential, and calculating the investment risk and rewards are all part of evaluating a potential deal.

We have a series of tasks we go through to evaluate potential deals.

This subject is more thoroughly covered in Chapter 5.

Risks of "Subject to" Mortgage Transactions

Despite the sexiness of "subject to" mortgage transactions, it is certainly not all glitz and glamour. Like any investment or financing strategy, there are clear benefits, but there are also business and financial risks in conducting such transactions.

Topics such as Due-on-Sale, Over-leveraging, Seller Interference, and Insurance are some of the risks common to "subject to" mortgage transactions.

This subject is more thoroughly covered in Chapter 6.

Due Diligence

As with any acquisition of investment property, we take steps to do a "due diligence" check. The term due diligence is a phrase for our thorough review of the status of the loan, the condition of the property, and a determination of any contingencies, such as unpaid liens on the property. Before we fully close on a property with a "subject to" mortgage, we must do our final due diligence check on the property, the loan, and the seller. It is the last major step before closing the deal.

We have a checklist of items we go through in our due diligence check and the things we look for.

This subject is more thoroughly covered in Chapter 7.

Closing the Deal

At the closing table, we have a set of expectations to ensure a smooth closing. We discuss and compare the surrounding issues of doing a bank closing, a "kitchen table" closing, and a traditional closing with a title company or real estate attorney.

We discuss what closing documents should be present at the closing. We have also included an overview on Land Trusts, which are legal instruments frequently used in conjunction with "subject to" mortgage transactions.

This subject is more thoroughly covered in Chapter 8.

After the Closing

After the closing, we have legal title to the property, but do we always get legal possession immediately? Unfortunately, we do not. We have to obtain legal possession quickly before issuing any payments to reinstate or to continue payments on the loan.

The lender and insurance companies have to be contacted and notified of the new mailing address and other administrative changes under the new management. There are follow-up tasks that we must do to convert this new acquisition into a profitable investment.

This subject is more thoroughly covered in Chapter 9.

Ongoing Issues

The inherent nature of a "subject to" mortgage transaction depends on successful management of the seller's loan. Over time, circumstances can change and people can change. What is the impact of those changes on a "subject to" mortgage transaction done years earlier? What are ongoing maintenance issues of "subject to" mortgage transactions? These are several issues of ongoing concern about which we must remain conscious of as the years progress.

This subject is more thoroughly covered in Chapter 10.

TurnKey Investing Philosophy

In all of our investments, we have an underlying management philosophy that guides our investment decisions and actions. We prefer to take a "turnkey" approach in everything we do. As such, we have developed a set of rules and guidelines we follow with our "Turnkey Investing Philosophy."

This subject is more thoroughly covered in Chapter 11.

Summary

Although the "subject to" mortgage transaction is conceptually easy to understand overall, what makes these transactions a challenge for many newer investors is the depth of understanding each component requires to make the entire transaction work. There are myriad issues and considerations that must be considered in conducting such transactions.

CHAPTER

3

Legitimizing "Subject to" Mortgage Transactions

There is a common saying that we use, "A confused mind will always say 'No'."

Few sayings are more accurate and appropriate than this one when it comes to discussing "subject to" mortgage transactions with an untrained and uninformed person, regardless of whether or not that person is a real estate professional.

Quite frankly, we keep our discussions of "subject to" mortgage transactions with people on a "need to know" basis. The whole concept of taking over a seller's loan without specific lender permission throws conservative thinkers off and immediately raises unnecessary panic and suspicions.

> *"If our business was sure-fire and guaranteed, it would not be called **investing**."*

As I will discuss, "subject to" mortgage transactions, like any other investment transactions, have their share of potential challenges and risks. But the business of investing is *risk management.* If our business was sure-fire and guaranteed, it would not be called investing.

A Personal Story

Over the last few years, I have on occasion told different friends, acquaintances, and even real estate professionals of how I bought property with a "subject to" mortgage. Of course, I would explain it as concisely as I could without the technical jargon.

I quickly discovered that the perception of what I was doing by those I told was very different from the reality. They saw me as "tricking" desperate sellers into giving me their property. In reality, I was making legal and legitimate offers to sellers (with whom nearly no one wanted to deal with) to buy their property with a form of seller-financing.

> *"Most people believe that the only way to buy any investment property is with new, conventional financing."*

Most people believe that the only way to buy any investment property is with new, conventional financing. Personally, I think it is a sad and limiting belief that I clearly do not subscribe to. It limits your mind and your ability to see and create opportunities.

Today, I simply tell acquaintances I buy property without giving any of the "interesting" details. It is too tiresome to educate the disinterested and cynical person. If you are reading this manual, you most likely do not qualify as being disinterested or cynical. You must have some level of belief in this concept to study and read this book.

No Man (or Woman) is an Island

Unfortunately, in the natural course of business, occasionally we have to deal with disinterested and cynical people and explain the legitimacy of what we do. After all, "no man (or woman) is an island." In our personal lives, we do not necessarily have to explain ourselves, but I have found that professionally, we occasionally do.

It is not enough to know how to conduct the "subject to" mortgage transaction. You occasionally have to be able to explain and, yes, justify the transaction to others – especially to real estate professionals you may encounter.

"It is not enough to know how to conduct the 'subject to' mortgage transaction."

Telling people you learned about the "subject to" mortgage from some real estate course or seminar is not generally a good way to earn credibility from the mainstream audience.

This is one of the biggest reasons I wrote this book, so that you, the reader, have a "legitimate" handbook and manual in your hands dedicated to "subject to" mortgages you can refer others to.

What I have discovered that can lend high credibility to your experience is to quote from reputable sources and books which actually explain the nature and intricacies of a "subject to" mortgage transaction.

In my research, I found it quite interesting just how many reputable and credible sources that the "subject to" mortgage appears.

For many, this one chapter will be worth more than the cost of this book. Normally, such information would be located in the Appendix at the back of the book. However, I feel the issue of legitimizing and building credibility concerning "subject to" mortgages is simply too important for anyone who plans to use the technique to ignore.

> *"For many, this one chapter will be worth more than the cost of this book."*

You will need this information if you encounter difficulties with bankers, lenders, appraisers, real estate agents, investors, attorneys, and insurance agents who may question the legitimacy of any "subject to" mortgage transaction you may do.

Driving Force for this Chapter

The driving force for me to write this book actually came from the need to "legitimize" the "subject to" mortgage transaction to those professionals with whom I had to deal with.

Although I knew "subject to" mortgages were perfectly legal and ethical because of the research I had personally done surrounding this subject, the local community which I worked in did not readily understand such unorthodox mortgages.

I grew tired of justifying what I did and re-explaining myself to the uninformed. In many ways, I have written this book for myself as much as I have for you, the reader.

I admit that it has been a slow process to get people to understand and embrace the "subject to" mortgage concept. It goes against what most people have been taught about property ownership, financing, and underlying mortgages.

However, over time I learned how to "legitimize" my transactions. What that means is that I can interact with most professionals without concern that they will think I am engaged in questionable business and investing practices.

With this handbook and manual, you now have a credible publication from which to "legitimize" any "subject to" mortgage transactions you do with your attorney, accountant, real estate broker, lender, and local authorities.

Over the last few years, I have made the effort and taken the time to assemble very important pieces of information that will help anyone who wants to engage in "subject to" mortgage transactions without the fear of suspicion or scrutiny.

In fact, I have no problem saying that this one chapter is worth ten times the cover price to be able to have the credibility and legitimacy to conduct such transactions.

Knowing and understanding how to buy investment property with a "subject to" mortgage is quite a bit different then selling the concept to a potential seller and, even more challenging, to conventional real estate practitioners.

Because "subject to" mortgage transactions are often taught in real estate seminars and courses as a sexy way of buying property with no money, no credit, and no partners, it carries with it a negative stigma by those who have not taken the time to learn and understand it.

"I believe there are some individuals who engage in these types of transactions when they have little clue as to the potential downside of these transactions."

Quite frankly, I believe there are some individuals who engage in these types of transactions when they have little clue as to the potential downside of these transactions. And you often hear of people who get into financial (and sometimes legal) trouble doing so.

Real Estate Attorneys

I recommend the following real estate attorneys for more information.

Bill Bronchick – Author & Colorado Real Estate Attorney

I hold Bill in high regard, and his credibility remains very high with me. When I first met him, he was a relatively unknown speaker who was instrumental to introducing me to many of the intricacies of using the "subject to" mortgage to buy properties.

Over the years he has since authored many books published by Dearborn Trade, a respected publisher. Bill has also appeared as a guest of CNBC. He has been featured in Money Magazine, USA Today, CNN Money, and the Denver Business Journal.

I also highly recommend his course "Alternative Real Estate Financing".

You can find Bill Bronchick at his website address, *http://www.legalwiz.com*.

Karen Earley – Georgia Real Estate Attorney

Karen, my real estate attorney, is a principal of *Meacham, Earley, and Fowler*, a respected law firm in our area. She is licensed in Illinois and Georgia. She does our real estate closings and gives high credibility to the "subject to" mortgage transactions we do.

Other Real Estate Attorneys

I know there are other real estate attorneys (and title companies) in the U.S. that understand "subject to" mortgage transactions. It is important that you seek them out to join your team in conducting "subject to" mortgage transactions. Having them as part of your team is almost mandatory to bring high credibility and legitimacy to any "subject to" mortgage transaction you might do.

Real Estate License Study Manuals

I found it interesting how often the term *"subject to" mortgage* came up in my research for this book. The "subject to" mortgage is clearly explained in several of the real estate sales license study guides. Yet, much of the resistance towards utilizing the "subject to" mortgage also comes from real estate agents that have allegedly read those study guides and passed the subsequent real estate license exams.

> *"Many real estate agents have forgotten what they allegedly read and studied on 'subject to' mortgage transactions."*

Apparently, many of those real estate agents have forgotten what they allegedly read and studied on "subject to" mortgage transactions. Either that, or they are simply in a state of denial.

Here are a few study guides to real estate licensing and investing that provide excellent advice on "subject to" mortgages:

Crawford, Linda J., *Florida Real Estate Exam Manual, 26th Edition.* Dearborn Financial Publishing. Chicago, Illinois, 2003.

Gallaty, Fillmore W., Allaway, Wellington J., & Kyle, Robert C. *Modern Real Estate Practice, 16th Edition.* Dearborn Financial Publishing. Chicago, Illinois, 2003.

Lindeman, J. Bruce & Friedman, Jack P. *How to Prepare for Florida Real Estate Exams: Salesperson, Broker, Appraiser.* Barron's Educational Services. Hauppauge, New York, 1997.

Martin, Joseph H. *Real Estate License Examinations, 5th Edition.* Thomson Learning. Lawrenceville, New Jersey, 2002.

Sterling, Joyce Bea. *Your Guide to Passing the AMP Real Estate Exam, 3rd Edition.* Dearborn Financial Publishing. Chicago, Illinois, 2001.

Tax Books

These well-established tax books cover "subject to" mortgage transactions for tax reporting purposes.

When buying one of these books, be sure to check for the latest edition, which should contain the most current information on "subject to" mortgage transactions.

Hoven, Vernon. *The Real Estate Investor's Tax Guide, 4th Edition.* Dearborn Financial Publishing. Chicago, Illinois, 2004.

J.K. Lasser's Your Income Tax 2004. J. K. Lasser Books, 2004.

General Real Estate Books

These well-respected real estate books contain information regarding "subject to" mortgages. However, I will admit, you have to truly want to research the topic to find it in these books. In each of these books, I presume later editions will also contain the most current information regarding "subject to" mortgage transactions.

Gadow, Sandy. *All About Escrow and Real Estate Closings, 6th Edition.* Escrow Publishing Co. Palm Beach, Florida, 1999.

Harris, Jack C. & Friedman, Jack P. *Real Estate Handbook, 5th Edition.* Barron's Educational Services. Hauppauge, New York, 2001.

Karp, James and Klayman, Elliot. *Real Estate Law, 5th Edition.* Dearborn Financial Publishing, Chicago, Illinois, 2003.

Nelson, Grant S. & Whitman, Dale A. *Real Estate Finance Law, 4th Edition.* West Law Books. St. Paul, Minnesota, 2003.

Settlement Statement

Perhaps the most compelling document I can offer you which proves that "subject to" mortgage transactions are legitimate, lawful, and ethical is a document that every U.S. closing attorney and title company uses for every property closing is the U.S. Housing and Urban Development Settlement Statement, often referred to as the "HUD-1 Settlement Statement."

The U.S. Department of Housing and Urban Development (HUD) developed this form for use throughout the U.S. for real estate closings between buyers and sellers.

(You can download an Adobe Acrobat PDF version from http://www.hudclips.org under the Forms Section of the website.)

This form provides a nationwide standard within which real estate closing agents use to document and disclose the numerous fees being charged and the monies being exchanged and paid as a result of a transaction.

In regards to "subject to" mortgages, there are specific line items:

- Under Section J, "Summary of Borrower's Transaction," line 203 is labeled *"Existing loan(s) taken subject to."*
- The corresponding entry under Section K, "Summary of Seller's Transaction," line 503 is labeled *"Existing loans taken subject to."*

Of all the resouces I have listed, the HUD-1 Settlement form is probably the most compelling proof to anyone within the U.S. that "subject to" mortgage

A. **Settlement Statement**

U.S. Department of Housing and Urban Development

OMB Approval No. 2502-0265 (expires 9/30/2006)

B. Type of Loan	6. File Number:	7. Loan Number:	8. Mortgage Insurance Case Number:
1. ☐ FHA 2. ☐ FmHA 3. ☐ Conv. Unins. 4. ☐ VA 5. ☐ Conv. Ins.			

C. Note: This form is furnished to give you a statement of actual settlement costs. Amounts paid to and by the settlement agent are show n. Items marked "(p.o.c.)" were paid outside the closing; they are shown here for informational purposes and are not included in the totals.

D. Name & Address of Borrower:	E. Name & Address of Seller:	F. Name & Address of Lender:

G. Property Location:	H. Settlement Agent:	
	Place of Settlement:	I. Settlement Date:

J. Summary of Borrower's Transaction		K. Summary of Seller's Transaction	
100. Gross Amount Due From Borrower		**400. Gross Amount Due To Seller**	
101. Contract sales price		401. Contract sales price	
102. Personal property		402. Personal property	
103. Settlement charges to borrower (line 1400)		403.	
104.		404.	
105.		405.	
Adjustments for items paid by seller in advance		**Adjustments for items paid by seller in advance**	
106. City/town taxes to		406. City/town taxes to	
107. County taxes to		407. County taxes to	
108. Assessments to		408. Assessments to	
109.		409.	
110.		410.	
111.		411.	
112.		412.	
120. Gross Amount Due From Borrower		**420. Gross Amount Due To Seller**	
200. Amounts Paid By Or In Behalf Of Borrower		**500. Reductions In Amount Due To Seller**	
201. Deposit or earnest money		501. Excess deposit (see instructions)	
202. ~~Principal amount of new loan(s)~~		502. ~~Settlement charges to seller~~ (line 1400)	
203. Existing loan(s) taken subject to		503. Existing loan(s) taken subject to	
204.		504. ~~Payoff of first mortgage loan~~	
205.		505. Payoff of second mortgage loan	
206.		506.	
207.		507.	
208.		508.	
209.		509.	
Adjustments for items unpaid by seller		**Adjustments for items unpaid by seller**	
210. City/town taxes to		510. City/town taxes to	
211. County taxes to		511. County taxes to	
212. Assessments to		512. Assessments to	
213.		513.	
214.		514.	
215.		515.	
216.		516.	
217.		517.	
218.		518.	
219.		519.	
220. Total Paid By/For Borrower		**520. Total Reduction Amount Due Seller**	
300. Cash At Settlement From/To Borrower		**600. Cash At Settlement To/From Seller**	
301. Gross Amount due from borrower (line 120)		601. Gross amount due to seller (line 420)	
302. Less amounts paid by/for borrower (line 220)	( )	602. Less reductions in amt. due seller (line 520)	( )
303. Cash ☐ From ☐ To Borrower		**603. Cash ☐ To ☐ From Seller**	

Section 5 of the Real Estate Settlement Procedures Act (RESPA) requires the following: ▯ HUD must develop a Special Information Booklet to help persons borrowing money to finance the purchase of residential real estate to better understand the nature and costs of real estate settlement services; ▯ Each lender must provide the booklet to all applicants from whom it receives or for whom it prepares a written application to borrow money to finance the purchase of residential real estate; ▯ Lenders must prepare and distribute with the Booklet a Good Faith Estimate of the settlement costs that the borrower is likely to incur in connection with the settlement. These disclosures are manadatory.

Section 4(a) of RESPA mandates that HUD develop and prescribe this standard form to be used at the time of loan settlement to provide full disclosure of all charges imposed upon the borrower and seller. These are third party disclosures that are designed to provide the borrower with pertinent information during the settlement process in order to be a better shopper.

The Public Reporting Burden for this collection of information is estimated to average one hour per response, including the time for reviewing instructions, searching existing data sources, gathering and maintaining the data needed, and completing and reviewing the collection of information.

This agency may not collect this information, and you are not required to complete this form, unless it displays a currently valid OMB control number. The information requested does not lend itself to confidentiality.

Previous editions are obsolete

Page 1 of 2

form **HUD-1** (3/86)
ref Handbook 4305.2

transactions are both legal and legitimate -- and recognized as such by the U.S. government. Most people simply have never paid attention to these line items because they were going through conventional financing procedures for obtaining new loans in which those line items 203 and 503 are not used.

Summary

We view the legitimization of our "subject to" mortgage transactions as a critical, essential, and ongoing process. Because the nature of such transactions are so unorthodox and goes against conventional wisdom and thinking, we take great care to ensure that our reputations remain high in the business and investment community.

CHAPTER

4

Finding the Urgent Seller

As I have mentioned earlier, there is a certain sexiness to buying property with a "subject to" mortgage. What's not to like? We get to buy property without qualifying for a mortgage. We simply "take over" the seller's loan where the seller retains the formal liability on the loan and yet we get the title.

Yet, this begs the question:

Why would sellers ever agree to a "subject to" mortgage?

This is probably the most often-asked question from non-investors and other people who do not understand the human side of deal-making.

They cannot comprehend how anyone could ever agree to a "subject to" mortgage or how anyone could give up ownership of their property but also maintain the liability of the mortgage. There are many reasons a seller wants to work with us.

We know that most people would never agree to this type of transaction if we, as buyers, made the offer to real estate agents and even most "For Sale By Owner" (FSBO) properties. As such, we change the dynamics between buyers and sellers.

> *"We directly market to potential sellers and have them call us."*

We directly market to potential sellers and have them call us!

Negotiation Dynamics are Changed

The dynamics of the negotiation are substantially altered when sellers call us. We then are in a position to ask questions about the property, their situation, their loan, and so forth. We easily and straight-forwardly obtain information that would normally not be disclosed in a conventional transaction.

If and when we determine that we are interested in the property and if the numbers work, we quickly ascertain whether the seller may be a good candidate for a "subject to" transaction by asking some probing questions as to their personal situation.

> *"The dynamics of the negotiation are substantially altered when sellers call us."*

We are looking for the "urgent seller." The urgent sellers are those homeowners with a high need to get rid of their property quickly. They do not want to wait for a conventional sale. In our local area, the average conventional home sale takes four months to complete. Remember, this is only an average. For every house that sells within two months, there is another house that takes six months to sell.

In that light, you might begin to realize how some sellers might eventually become "urgent sellers." Their patience, time, or money runs out. Gradually, they become more receptive to alternative options that may not be ideal but which still serve their need to dispose of the property.

Circumstances Creating Urgent Sellers

The actual circumstances of the seller can be many. We have encountered sellers in different situations that create a sense of urgency to sell:

- Job Relocation
- Separation or Divorce
- Retirement
- Impending Foreclosure
- Deficient Property Condition
- Behind Payments
- Little or No Equity

Frequently, an immediate or impending financial distress causes our sellers to take an **active** role in the selling process. For those people, waiting for a conventional sale through a real estate agent is unrealistic or may simply come too late to be of help.

Without circumstances that create an urgent seller, there is little need or desire for a "subject to" mortgage transaction to occur.

> *"We are never the 'ideal' solution, and we tell them so."*

We then offer an alternative solution. We are never the "ideal" solution, and we tell them so. The "ideal" solution for most sellers is, of course, for a buyer to come in with all-new financing to fully cash out the seller and satisfy the existing mortgage.

Job Relocation

In our area, we have a major Army base, Ft. Benning. Often, Army personnel are given orders to quickly transfer and move out of the area. When that occurs, unless they are well-positioned financially, these new sellers have to sell on a deadline that no real estate agent can guarantee.

Separation or Divorce

In any community, there are incidents of separation or divorce. Often, it is not the separation or divorce that requires a home to be sold. It is the fact that half the income source that was needed to support the household has left. One spouse's income is sometimes not enough to support the household and they are compelled to sell their home.

Retirement

We had a married couple who simply wanted to retire quickly and move on without the burden of preparing their home for resale. Although, they had equity, they simply wanted the convenience of moving on with little work.

Impending Foreclosure

Quite often, an impending or imminent foreclosure is a compelling reason for homeowners to sell. However, the wait time for a conventional sale is often too long and will not stop an imminent foreclosure. Whether the property has equity or not is irrelevant. The fact that foreclosure is only weeks away is. Without a new buyer and a large and quick infusion of funds to reinstate the loan, there is no way to stop a foreclosure. We often are that last resort.

Deficient Property Condition

Poor or deficient property condition often creates a selling dilemma for homeowners who want to sell and move. These properties command a low market price in "as is" condition and to get a higher market price often requires investing more money into the property for repairs and maintenance. This is often a financial burden and inconvenience many sellers cannot bear. Additionally, most real estate agents are unwilling to devote much of their time to deficient properties when they have many nicer properties to sell with larger commissions to earn.

Behind Payments

Closely related to impending foreclosure, these sellers are not in immediate danger of foreclosure but they are in the early stages of mounting debt and loan arrearage. Their credit and account are delinquent. These sellers realize that if they do not take action quickly, the situation will quickly worsen and they want someone to step in to help them out of the situation.

Little or No Equity

Regardless of condition, properties with little or no equity are difficult to sell because there is little room for price negotiation even if the seller was willing to discount. The amount owed on a property is too close to the actual market value of the property. Real estate agents do not like these properties because there is not enough equity within the property for them to easily collect their sales commissions from the sellers. Homeowners in this position are often left to fend for themselves with few easy options.

Finding the Urgent Seller

A frequently asked question is:

If sellers who will sell with a "subject to" mortgage are so rare, how do you find them?

The answer is simple. **We advertise for them!**

We regularly advertise in the Real Estate section of the city newspaper. We also advertise regularly in the local American Classifieds, a FREE classifieds-only newspaper. A similar paper in other parts of the country is the PennySaver, which publishes editions in local communities in many states. We have used this advertising plan for several years, and it generates many leads for us to follow. Of course, we cannot help most sellers who call us, but we do not need many to make it financially worthwhile for us to advertise.

One magical phrase we use in our ads tells it all: **"We buy houses fast!"**

We prominently include our website address: **http://www.prohomebuyers.com** and our phone number in all of our advertisements.

People are more familiar with us through our sister site: **http://www.ownerfinancehomes.com** for people who want to buy our houses.

Winning Sellers Over

When we meet with sellers, there are two major areas of discussion we focus on.

We simultaneously sell ourselves as *credible buyers* and we focus on the *seller's benefits.*

We sell ourselves on:

- Rapport
- Trust
- Confidence
- Credibility
- Financial Ability
- Performance – Fast and Easy
- No Commissions

When we are negotiating with the seller and as we speak with them, we have to sell ourselves and our company to them. Unfortunately, a lot of what sells ourselves cannot be easily explained in this handbook. Much of it is in our interpersonal interactions with the sellers.

Rapport

We always first try to establish a rapport with the sellers. I give credit to my partner, Wes Weaver, for doing an excellent job of building an empathetic relationship with the sellers. I think he does a much better job than I do in creating rapport. Nevertheless, I do my part in creating rapport by carefully listening to the sellers and addressing their needs.

Trust

As we build rapport, we move towards building a sense of trust. Part of this trust is based on building our credibility. We discuss our past experience in this arena as well as the network of professionals we work with (such as our insurance agent and real estate attorney) who assist us in supporting what we do. My management partner, Wes Weaver, and I often use a tag-team approach in this regard.

Confidence

At all times we project unwavering confidence that we can do what we say we can do. Confidence is compelling, and sellers seem to take comfort in our knowledge, expertise, and experience as we guide them through the process and answer their questions in a direct and straightforward manner.

Credibility

As seller discussions continue, we are careful to drop in credibility statements of our knowledge, experience, and expertise. We let sellers know we have a network of professionals at our disposal that support what we do. This includes our real estate attorney, insurance agent, and contractors.

Financial Ability

We try not to be too detailed about this point, but we inform them that we have financial resources that go beyond ourselves that includes business associates and investment partners. We provide this information to let them know that we have the financial wherewithal to ride out any bad times we may encounter as we pay on their loan.

Performance

We inform sellers of our success history and our ability to perform quickly and professionally – that it is a simple matter of our inspecting the property, looking over their loan papers, verifying the loan status, and then going to our real estate attorney to close the deal.

No Commissions

We tell them we do not work on commissions. When we buy property, we are in it for the long haul. We do not intend to buy the house and simply leave, abandon the property, and hurt our personal reputations along the way. We are committed to the property (and their loan) through good times and bad times, which is the reason that we don't earn our money through commissions.

Focusing on Seller's Benefits

We focus on benefits to the seller:

- Avoiding Long Sales Period
- Immediate Debt Relief
- No Closing Costs
- Little or No Equity is Acceptable
- Will Buy in "As Is" Condition
- Quick Funds
- No Commissions

If we are interested in buying a seller's property with a "subject to" mortgage, there are stages of selling the idea of such a mortgage to them. We focus on the issues that most directly impact the sellers.

Avoiding Long Sales Period

In our area, the average days-on-the-market for any given property is four months. We inform the seller that some properties sell within two months, but an equal number of properties take six months to sell, thus creating the four-month average. We let them consider for themselves where in that spectrum their house will fall and how we can help them avoid a long sales period.

Immediate Debt Relief

Regardless of whether a seller is in arrears, if they are in the process of moving, they want to be released from mortgage payment obligations. Immediate release of the weight of their debt is often an important reason for them to sell to us on a "subject to" mortgage.

> *"Immediate release of the weight of their debt is often an important reason for them to sell to us."*

We inform them that we can start making their mortgage payments almost immediately after they decide to move and after they complete the paperwork on the sale with us.

No Closing Costs

We inform the sellers that we pay all out-of-pocket costs with the closing attorney. They will pay no fees whatsoever for completing a "subject to" mortgage transaction.

Little or No Equity is Acceptable

We bring up the fact that unless they are prepared to go through the trouble of selling the house themselves, few real estate agents will volunteer to sell their little or no equity house unless the sellers are willing to pay the realtor's large sales commission out of their own pockets.

By the time they get to us, they often feel quite abandoned by the traditional real estate agent community. We are generally the only ones able to provide them a truly workable solution.

We reassure our sellers that our buying property with little or no equity is quite acceptable as long as the the initial loan terms and monthly loan payment is low enough for us to maintain.

Will Buy in "As Is" Condition

We ask sellers, "How many people would be willing to buy their property in "as is" condition?" especially if the property was well lived in and obviously shows wear and tear from that occupancy. In fact, many real estate agents often demand that sellers fix up their homes before they will even consider trying to sell it.

> *"We inform them that we have to make a profit in buying their house so we cannot offer full price."*

If we can make the numbers work, we generally buy property in "as is" condition and accept the responsibilities for defects and deficiencies we find.

Quick Funds

If they have a good amount of equity in their property, we can offer some quick funds for their house. However, we inform them that we have to make a profit in buying their house so we cannot offer full price. In any case, they would have to pay a 7% commission from their equity for a real estate agent to sell their property, so they would never see that portion of their equity. Also, if they factored in vacancy costs, they would probably give up another 3% in equity to pay for it. In that case, it might be easier for them to sell their property quickly to us at a discount.

No Commissions

We tell them they are not being charged agent commissions dealing with us. If they had sold through a real estate agent, they would have to pay a large sales commission to someone who would have little financial interest beyond the sale. Whereas, we have an ongoing financial interest long after the sale.

> *"We have an ongoing financial interest long after the sale."*

Our Responses to Seller's Concerns

As you might expect, even if we encounter an urgent seller and earn their trust, there are seller concerns that arise to which we have to respond.

- How do I know you will make my loan payments?
- What will you do with the property?
- What if the property is ruined?
- How long will the loan be in my name?
- Are you sure this is legal?
- Can I consult my attorney?
- Can I lease the property back from you?
- What if the lender calls the loan due?
- Why don't you get a new loan to buy my house?

Below are our typical responses to questions they direct to us.

How do I know you will make my loan payments?

I understand your concern. I would also be concerned if I were in your place. You can be assured we will make steady payments because we are not in the business of losing houses. If we do not pay, we won't have the house for very long because the lender will foreclose on the property. Does it make sense we would put our time, effort, and money into this property only to let the lender take the house back? Additionally, we have personal reputations in our community to protect.

What will you do with the property?

There are not too many things we can do with the property. We will either resell the property or lease it. More than likely, we will lease the property out to a tenant who is ultimately interested in purchasing the property. That tenant will ideally lease the property for two years and then qualify for refinancing. However, we may have to go through a few tenants over the next few years because not all tenants are successful in obtaining refinancing.

> *"We have personal reputations in our community to protect."*

No matter what happens with the tenant, we are ultimately responsible for the property.

What if the property is ruined?

Because you are selling the property to us, we will have financial, management, maintenance, and repair responsibilities. You no longer have any headaches to worry about. In any case, it is in our best interest for us to find the best tenant possible and do a good job managing the property to preserve the value of the house.

How long will the loan be in my name?

It is difficult to say, but you can believe it is also in our best interest to have our tenants cash the property out. After all, we get most of our profits when the property cashes out, not letting it sit month after month making a couple of hundred dollars a month.

We will do everything we can to have the loan cashed out, but we cannot guarantee when that will occur because our tenants must have sufficient time to live in the house, clean up their credit, and qualify for the loan. Sometimes, tenants don't work out, and we may have to put in another tenant, starting the cycle again.

> *"If it were illegal, do you think our real estate attorney would close the transaction for us?"*

What you can be sure of is that your credit will improve over time because we will continue making mortgage payments, and you will receive the credit for our great payment record.

Are you sure this is legal?

I am absolutely certain this transaction is entirely legal. If it weren't legal, our real estate attorney would not close these transactions for us. The money they make on the closing fee is not worth losing their license to practice law. Additionally, when we get to the closing table, you will find that the HUD-1 statement actually lists this type of transaction in one of the line items. If it were illegal, do you think our real estate attorney would close the transaction for us? For that matter, would there be a line entry on the HUD-1 statement indicating this kind of transaction?

Can I consult my attorney?

Yes, you may. But you may want to ask yourself, in the event that your attorney advises against it, what will you do? It is easy for someone to say to you should not sell this way, but will that person offer you a good alternative? Who will continue making payments if you can't afford it? Are they willing to step in and make the payments for you and take full responsibility for the property as we will?

Can I lease the property back from you?

Unfortunately, company policy prevents us from doing that. If we buy a property, the seller has to move out. It prevents any future conflicts of interest.

What if the lender calls the loan due?

That is a great question. In our experience, we find that lenders hate having loans get behind on payments. They want people to continue making payments. In fact, I have actually spoken to foreclosure attorneys about this issue, and the last thing that any lender wants to do is foreclose on a loan. Lenders prefer that the borrower find a way to save the loan.

Today, there are so many people losing homes to foreclosure. We rarely hear of any lenders looking to deliberately ruin a borrower's credit or force anyone into foreclosure – especially not on a loan that is current and performing.

However, in the unlikely event that the lender insists on calling the loan due, my partner and I, or one of our business associates, would qualify for the existing loan or a new loan so that a foreclosure would not occur.

Why don't you get a new loan to buy my house?

If we had to get a new loan to buy your house, it would add thousands of dollars to the purchase price of the house, which would no longer make it financially worthwhile for us to buy.

> *"We rarely hear of any lenders looking to deliberately ruin a borrower's credit or force anyone into foreclosure."*

If we have to qualify for a new loan, we would probably look at another property at a better price or better condition. There would be little incentive for us to buy your house with a new loan unless it is well discounted.

Summary

No matter how savvy and how much technical knowledge we have, we know a "subject to" mortgage transaction always comes down to finding the suitable urgent seller, establishing our credibility, and earning their trust. The act of dealing with urgent sellers is more of an art than a science because of the often unpredictable human factor. This obviously improves with our ongoing experience.

CHAPTER

5

Evaluating Potential Deals

Through our marketing efforts, we get a steady flow of potential sellers who want to sell their houses to us. They do not initially know we are interested in buying their properties with a "subject to" mortgage until we pre-screen them first.

Once we determine that the seller may be a good candidate and agreeable to a "subject to" mortgage transaction, we immediately move to look at the financials to evaluate the potential returns and profitability of the property.

> *"We immediately move to look at the financials to evaluate potential returns and profitability of the property."*

Naturally, all investors want to buy property with the most equity at the best interest rates. We are certainly no different in this regard.

In evaluating a potential "subject to" mortgage transaction, we look to the following factors to evaluate the deal:

- How much are the monthly payments? What are our rewards for taking on that risk?
- How much "real equity" is there?
- How much "potential equity" can be converted into "real equity"?
- Is the loan in arrears? If so, how much is owed? Has it gone to the foreclosure attorney?

The chart that follows shows our basic checklist of factors we consider in deciding on whether a deal will be profitable.

Seller Information Sheet

Phone

Seller Name: ______________________ Home #: ____________

Address: ______________________ Work #: ____________

City/State/ZIP: ______________________ Mobile #: ____________

#BR / #BA: ____________ Square Footage: ____________

How long Occupied: ____________ Age of Property: ____________

Property Status: Owner-occupied / Rental / Vacant

Condition of Property: Excellent / Good / Fair / Poor

Repairs & Maintenance Needed: ______________________________

Seller's FMV: $____________

Our FMV: $____________

1st Lender: ______________________________

Monthly Pymt: $____________ Balance: $ ____________

Arrearage: $____________ Interest: ________%

2nd Lender: ______________________________

Monthly Pymt: $____________ Balance: $ ____________

Arrearage: $____________ Interest: ________%

Reason for Selling: ______________________

Cash seller Needs: $____________

Planned Move Date: ____________

Monthly Payments

The most important criterion we look for in a "subject to" mortgage transaction is the amount of the monthly payments. This amount is important for two reasons. First, the monthly payment amount helps determine our overall risk and ability to hold on to the property. Even if the property has equity, should it become financially impractical to support the monthly payment amount, we have to take that cash flow issue into consideration.

> *"The other important reason for looking at the monthly payment is to determine whether we can profit from the monthly cash flow."*

The other important reason for looking at the monthly payment is to determine whether we can profit from the monthly cash flow. More specifically, how much of a monthly "spread" (profit) can we make between market rents we receive from a lease-option tenant (our specialty) and the seller's loan payment? And if we can get a "good" monthly spread (over $200.00), is it feasible for us to carry that property when it is vacant?

For example, obligating ourselves to taking on a loan with a $500 monthly mortgage payment to earn a $200 monthly spread is far more attractive than taking on a loan with a $1,500 monthly mortgage payment to earn the same spread. The monthly risk of the second scenario is triple that of the first scenario for the same reward.

Having a lower monthly payment relative to what we can get from lease-option market rent gives us the ability to profit from a little or no-equity property.

Taking it further, evaluating the monthly mortgage payment to what we could get from a conventional rental would give us a more conservative view of our ability to profit.

Real Equity

Although it does not happen frequently, I have bought property that already had "real equity" positions (over 15%). In one case, the seller could not tap into that equity because he was too far in arrears to save the property, and foreclosure was imminent. In another case, the cost of repairing the central air-conditioning unit was too great for the seller to overcome.

> *"We generally view properties with less than 10% equity as 'paper equity'."*

In both cases, after I stepped in and purchased the property with a "subject to" mortgage, I fixed the problem areas by making up the loan arrearage, thereby reinstating the loan, then paid for the necessary repairs. Once I completed those steps, I had over 20% of real equity in both properties.

We generally view properties with less than 10% equity as "paper equity". We say "paper equity" because it has a way of quickly vanishing when setbacks occur. It is the equity many beginning investors and non-investors view as "real equity" when often we view it as "paper equity."

Potential Equity

In one of our "subject to" mortgage transactions, we bought a property that was well outside of our normal buying parameters. The property was barely in move-in condition and a candidate for a renovation project. My management partner, Wes, and I debated the pros and cons of buying the property to renovate. After some discussion, we agreed we did not want to enter the renovation business, especially for only one property.

However, we did feel that there was a good amount of potential equity to be realized if we could find a knowledgeable handyman tenant who could do the renovations. We would be willing to have a very small monthly spread in exchange for the right tenant. After a couple of failed attempts to find the right tenant, I am happy to report we found a good tenant who has significantly renovated the property, and we are well on our way to converting the potential equity we saw into real equity.

Secondarily, by looking at the amortization schedule, we knew the remaining life of the loan was short enough that principal paydown would rapidly occur each month increasing our equity position.

Loan Arrearages

> *"How many real estate agents would step in to buy their property, make up their loan arrearages, and then continue to pay on a vacant property?"*

As you might expect, people who have loan arrearages are especially agreeable to someone taking over their loan, particularly if foreclosure is imminent. The downside to this deal is that some sellers are not especially informed or educated about property sales. In many cases, the loan arrearages are an unfortunate by-product of a job layoff or financial mismanagement. The seller realizes that he can no longer afford the property and lets the loan fall into arrears.

Some sellers understand that time is of the essence, and that they need to move out quickly and have someone, such as ourselves, step in and take over their payments. When we meet these types of sellers who still have a sense of responsibility, we feel we provide an invaluable service. After all, how many real estate agents would step in to buy their property, make up their loan arrearages, and then continue to pay on a vacant property?

Recently, I had a discussion on this very issue with the director of a servicing agency while trying to resolve loan issues. I asked her if they preferred to have the property go into foreclosure because we could still arrange for that to occur by simply ceasing all payments to them.

"We also encounter foolish sellers that try to abuse the system."

However, despite her grumblings of how we didn't "ask permission" before taking over the loan, she made it clear that letting the payments and property go was not something they could or would encourage us to do. The bottom line is that they much preferred a loan that was current and performing.

When sellers have the urgency to move and have us take over their loan, we do our best to accommodate them. Not only does it give them financial and mental relief but also it makes our financial position stronger not to let the loan incur any more late fees than necessary.

Unfortunately, we also encounter foolish sellers that try to abuse the system. They fall into arrears and, of course, they are interested in selling their property, having us take over their loans, and pay their loan arrearages. Naturally, we inform them that time is of the essence and their loan arrearages will get worse, making it more difficult for us to justify the purchase.

In their minds, they only see that we are interested in buying their property with some degree of urgency. What they fail to understand even after we explain the situation to them is that if the loan arrearages are too great, everyone loses. The lender has a non-performing loan which must be foreclosed, the seller's credit is ruined, and we lose an investment opportunity.

> *"There is a limit to how much we are willing to make up in loan arrearages."*

We have had sellers who waited too long. In their greed to "milk the property" by staying the extra month or two without payments, they lost any chance of our saving them from foreclosure. They had let the loan arrearages mount too high for us to be interested in the property any more. They became a foreclosure statistic. In these situations, I have no remorse and they entirely deserve what happens to them. After all, the foreclosure could have been prevented if they simply stopped milking the property to its demise.

While buying property with a "subject to" mortgage can overcome many financial hurdles, there is a limit to how much we are willing to make up in loan arrearages. Too much cash buried into a deal with little equity makes no sense to us, so we walk away from those deals which require too much cash to reinstate.

Foreclosure Attorney

When a lender has exhausted its efforts to collect from the borrower, the loan will be sent to a foreclosure attorney to begin foreclosure proceedings. As buyers, if we want to buy the property with a "subject to" mortgage at that point, we will have to deal with the foreclosure attorney.

We do not like having to deal with the foreclosure attorney because we know that the reinstatement fee will be much more than the principal, interest, and late fees the seller owes. There will be substantial penalty fees, as well as attorney fees, which have to be paid before the foreclosure attorney will stop the proceedings.

> *"When the deal is being handled by the foreclosure attorney, we do not have the luxury of an extended evaluation period."*

Generally, there are not many options for us except to try to negotiate down some of the attorney fees in exchange for overnight payment. We then take the reinstatement amount given to us and evaluate whether it will be profitable for us to do the deal. We also take into consideration how much time we have to reinstate the loan.

If the time frame is less than a week, there is very little we can do to save the seller because it takes almost a week to have the title checked and to set up an appointment for closing. The exception to that time limit is if the foreclosure attorney informs us that there is clear title and the seller can move out almost immediately. Then we can arrange for a quick closing.

When the deal is being handled by the foreclosure attorney, we do not have the luxury of an extended evaluation period.

Vacancy Cost

Even if there are no loan arrearages, every investment property has a vacancy cost. The reason here for that is that the seller must first move out before we can do anything with the property. The time it takes after the seller moves out for us to prepare the property, market the property, and ultimately resell it is the vacancy cost.

We never let the seller stay. It creates a conflict of interest for us if the seller stays. Therefore, we always have a vacancy cost that must be taken into consideration.

Marketing Costs

Nearly every property we buy with a "subject to" mortgage has marketing costs. More specifically, these are costs related to advertising. Occasionally, we get lucky, and a buyer who was looking at another one of our houses is interested in the new property we are about to acquire. Sometimes they like the house, and we never had to incur the expense of advertising the house.

Property Preparation Expenses

Nearly every property we buy has property preparation expenses. What we mean by property preparation expenses are those services that we hire out to make the property saleable.

For example, we prepare our properties to sell on a lease-option. There are things we do to prepare every property for sale. We hire a housekeeper to clean the house. That might include wiping down all the surfaces, cleaning the bathrooms and kitchen, trash removal, vacuuming, and mopping.

We sometimes hire our handyman to make minor repairs such as leaky faucets, toilets, and other smaller improvements that increase the perceived value of the house. We also hire a yard person to mow the loan, trim the bushes, sweep the porch, and basically make sure the exterior of the property looks clean.

The specifics of what we do to prepare a property are in a previous book, *TurnKey Investing with Lease-Options.*

Homestead Exemption Status

Nearly every property we buy with a "subject to" mortgage transaction initially falls within homestead exemption status. Homestead exemption allows the property owner (who occupies the property as their primary residence) a tax break with regards to their property taxes. This homestead exemption must be renewed annually.

When we take over the property, we know this fact and we take that into account that it will impact the escrow portion of our monthly P.I.T.I. (principal, interest, taxes, insurance) payments. We expect that the monthly payments will increase. The anticipated monthly payment must also allow for us to be profitable for us to consider completing the transaction.

Deal Evaluation Formulas

These are the basic formulas we use to evaluate potential "subject to" mortgage deals.

To calculate the estimated purchase price, we using the following formula.

Purchase Price =

Loan Balance + Loan Arrearage + Reinstatement or Late Fees + Seller Cash + Closing Costs

To the astute reader, it is clear that when we make up arrearages, some of that money actually goes towards principal. We are not interested in precise numbers. We are evaluating the overall deal. If the deal does not work because of a $200 purchase price difference, then the deal is too unforgiving and should not be pursued any further.

To calculate our upfront cash investment on the property, we use the following:

Upfront Cash =

Loan Arrearage + Reinstatement or Late Fees + Seller Cash + Vacancy Cost + Closing Costs

There actually are minor cash costs including housekeeping, minor repairs, and maintenance that factor in. Unless they become significant, we use the simpler formula.

We determine the estimate monthly cash flow with:

Monthly Cash Flow =

Market Rent – Monthly payment

Please keep in mind that these are only basic financial tools we use to evaluate the entire deal.

Making the Offer

If we do our jobs well as negotiators and educators concerning the "subject to" mortgage concept, the sellers will be agreeable to moving forward. In that case, we move to formalize the offer by writing up a purchase and sales contract.

Purchase & Sales Contract

We use a customized Purchase and Sales Contract which is specifically designed to accommodate "subject to" mortgage terms, simply as a matter of convenience for ourselves. However, you will be able to use most standard purchase and sales contracts which allow for buying property with assumable mortgages. You simply have to make a few changes to the paragraph that deals with loan assumptions. The specific changes will depend on the contract you have and the wording being used.

For people who are unaccustomed to modifying contracts as we are, you will want to consult your real estate attorney.

Remember, we are *not* formally assuming a mortgage, but we consider what we do as assuming a non-assumable mortgage. The end result is the same. The deal is being done with the existing loan.

If and when we decide we are interested in buying a property and the sellers are agreeable to our terms, we have them sign our purchase and sales contract. We submit the signed purchase and sales contract to our real estate attorney to prepare our closing.

Summary

Evaluating potential "subject to" mortgage deals always require us to know how we intend to ultimately profit from the investment. This often requires careful forethought and consideration. Gathering the right information and then evaluating the financial snapshot is essential for us to decide whether any further steps should be taken.

CHAPTER

6

The Risks of "Subject to" Mortgage Transactions

Let me start this chapter by saying that if we did not find it advantageous or if we did not like doing "subject to" mortgage transactions, we certainly would not engage in this work, much less spend time writing about it in this book. And while there is risk for every "subject to" mortgage transaction we do, the same can also be said of any investment transaction.

I want to be clear that there **are** risks in doing "subject to" mortgage transactions. However, there are risks in *any* kind of real estate investment. You simply have to know what risks you are willing to assume and which ones you are not. Anyone who says that any type of investing has **no** risk is either misleading people or misrepresenting the facts. The question we then have to ask ourselves is, "Can we accept the risks associated with the transaction?"

> *"I want to be clear that there **are** risks in doing 'subject to' mortgage transactions."*

Obviously, the short answer is "yes" because we continue to do "subject to" mortgage transactions. But because the intent of this book is to educate, I will delve into the various areas of risk as I see them. There are several of them.

- Over-Leverage
- Original Borrower Demands a Cash-Out
- Lack Of Professional Support
- Seller Interference With Lender

- Seller Interference With Property
- Insurance
- Doctrine of Implied Assumption
- Due-On-Sale Clause

Over-Leverage

One of the benefits of doing a "subject to" mortgage transaction is that it *potentially* allows you to easily buy any property a seller is willing to sell you. The downside is that there are many properties which would be financially suicidal to purchase even if you bought them with a "subject to" mortgage. It is very common to encounter sellers with highly leveraged or over-leveraged properties.

> *"The downside is that there are many properties which would be financially suicidal to purchase even if you bought them with a 'subject to' mortgage."*

When we encounter sellers with loans at a relatively low interest rate (8% or lower), even if the property has no equity, we are confident we can make it profitable. And we do! So, it follows if the property even has some small amount of equity, it is a no-brainer to buy the property with a "subject to" mortgage. We are highly leveraged in the property (up to 100%), but we also are comfortable with taking on and making the monthly payments. Without the closing costs and qualification hassles of a new loan, we can justify taking on that amount of leverage.

At the other end of the spectrum I have encountered distressed sellers who had mortgage loans of up to 13% interest with no equity, who were desperately pleading with me to take over payments on their houses. I can safely say that taking on a house with an interest rate of over 10% with little or no equity in the property is no deal at all.

> *"Building a portfolio of properties with high interest rate loans and little or no equity is a surefire way to end anyone's investment career."*

Building a portfolio of properties with high interest rate loans and little or no equity is a surefire way to end anyone's investment career. Without a low monthly payment, there is almost no way to profitably sustain the property month after month.

As you might guess, there are other deals that come our way which are not so clear cut. They are *borderline deals.* They have little equity and the payments are only marginally low. With these borderline deals, we have to look beyond the numbers and rely on our experience and intuitive sense as to whether we can truly make the deal work over the long term. And if the deal does not perform well, we must consider whether we will be able to sustain it.

Although there are properties we buy which have either real or potential equity, there are many more which do not. We have to ask ourselves with each property we buy how leveraged we are. If there is a downturn or extended vacancy, we may find ourselves over-leveraged. That is a risk of doing "subject to" mortgage transactions.

Original Borrower Demands a Cash-Out

When we buy the property with a "subject to" mortgage and take over the seller's loan, the loan remains on the seller's credit report. And while we take great care and time to explain to the seller that the loan will be on their credit report for an indefinite amount of time, we run the risk that they will conveniently "forget" what we told them as the years progress – or they may get impatient and want the loan satisfied.

> *"We run the risk that they will conveniently 'forget' what we told them as the years progress."*

Another issue with the seller's credit is that having the loan on their credit record may inhibit their ability to buy another property should they decide to years down the road. If it inhibits their ability to buy another home, they may become unhappy with the arrangement. Fortunately, a signed letter for their new lenders indicating that our company is making the monthly payments often overcomes such concerns.

Or as the years go on, our seller may simply tire of having their loan sit on their credit report indefinitely. We feel confident it is not a major concern but it is still a risk nonetheless.

Lack of Professional Support

Because very few people understand the "subject to" mortgage transaction, it can create confusion and a negative reaction by some of the professionals you may need as part of your team. I have heard uninformed people refer to the transaction as an illegal one, which is, of course, simply untrue.

For example, having an insurance agent who understands the transaction is necessary to write the policy correctly so that our interests and those of the seller and lender are all simultaneously protected.

"Although some people may disagree, I consider investment and financial partners an essential part of the team."

Early on, I did my own closings at the bank with sellers. Each time I did those closings, I was always a bit nervous, concerned that I might make an error which would hinder or even stop the closing. Also, despite the fact that we closed at the banks, there was no objective third party to conduct the closing. As such, our earlier closings lacked the credibility our later ones do.

Although some people may disagree, I consider investment and financial partners an essential part of the team. On a personal level, my credit standing and access to financial resources allows me a financial buffer should a "subject to" transaction "go bad." However, I also realize that there is a limit to how much financial risk I alone can assume. This is one important reason I work with Wes Weaver, my management partner.

> *"Doing 'subject to' mortgage transactions* ***without*** *a good professional support team is very risky indeed and equivalent to playing with a loaded gun."*

Together, our network of contacts and investment partners allows us the peace of mind to continually do "subject to" mortgage transactions. If any of them "go bad," we have many contacts we can turn to who are more than willing to buy into the great deals that we do.

In my view, doing "subject to" mortgage transactions even with a team of professionals to support us already has certain risks. Doing "subject to" mortgage transactions **without** a good professional support team is very risky indeed and equivalent to playing with a loaded gun.

Seller Interference with Lender

A risk that we try to get in front of early in our negotiations is not having our sellers interfere with our relationship with the lender.

When we deal with lenders, we position ourselves as property managers whom have full authority to conduct any or all transactions necessary to maintain the profitable performance of the property. We do this with written instruments such as Letter of Authorization and Power of Attorney.

> *"Many people associate having their name on the mortgage as their claim of ownership."*

Nevertheless, the loan remains in the seller's name. As such, the seller at any time has the ability to override what we have set in place. They can make account changes, solicit information, and redirect correspondence.

This is something we are quite cautious about. We try to frame it with the seller that we cannot do our jobs if we do not get information. And we cannot make timely payments if we do not receive payment books or statements. Of course, we subtly let them know that their credit record is also at stake if we cannot easily do our jobs.

Seller Interference with Property

Despite our best efforts to educate our sellers, a risk of doing "subject to" mortgage transactions is that they conveniently "forget" they have sold the property. Many people associate having their name on the mortgage as their claim of ownership. The truth of the matter is that "ownership" of a property is actually separate from "being liable" for the mortgage.

We make it as clear as possible to the seller that once the paperwork is signed, they no longer have any say in the management of the property.

The risk with the sellers is that unless they truly believe and understand it, they can still interfere with how we manage the property, especially if they want to continue inspecting the property when we are working to have tenants placed in the property.

Seller Wants the Property Back

Closely related to the issue of confusing one's name on a loan with actual ownership of the property is the risk that a seller may want his property back. My partner and I live in an area where property values appreciate slowly. When we buy little or no equity properties, there is relatively little danger that a seller will want the property back. After all, unless the seller has sentimental ties to a particular property, there is almost no financial incentive to retrieve the property.

Many have sold their property to us because they could no longer afford it. That negative experience will prevent many from wanting to move back to that same property even if they have financially recovered.

However, I have heard from associates and investor friends living in areas where property values appreciate rapidly – California is one such area – sellers sometimes try to retrieve the property they sold. These sellers make all kinds of outrageous accusations such as that the transaction was fraudulent, that they did not know what they were doing, that they still own the property because the mortgage is still in their name, or that they were tricked into the sale.

What has occurred in these areas is that the sellers realize that the high appreciation of properties in their area has generated huge equity positions in the property they sold. And they have 'seller's remorse', so they try to get the property back because the mortgage is still in their name.

"I dislike and highly recommend against 'kitchen table' closings."

As you might expect, my investor friends are outraged by these accusations because many bought the property when the seller was financially distressed, in arrears, and non-performing on loan repayment. The sellers want the property back after the house in good repair and the loan is current.

It is because of this concern that I dislike and highly recommend against "kitchen table" closings – where the buyer and seller sit down together (usually at the seller's home) to complete the deal – and highly recommend closing with a well-established real estate attorney or title company. More on this in a later chapter.

Property Insurance

I have several investor friends throughout the country who also buy properties with "subject to" mortgages. And the common challenge (and risk) is that there seem to be variations on how the insurance policy should be written to properly cover everyone's interest.

There is no disputing the fact that at least three parties' interests should be covered: ours, the lender's, and the seller's. However, the recommended way this protection is incorporated into the insurance policy can vary from agent to agent, and carrier to carrier.

> *"There is no disputing the fact that at least three parties' interests should be covered: ours, the lender's, and the seller's."*

For example, the lender is clearly listed as the mortgagee. What is not consistently clear is who the primary "named insured" should be -- us or the seller. To complicate matters further, we place title to our properties into corporate entities and/or land trusts for asset protection.

Many insurance agents claim that insurers prefer to cover individuals, not corporate entities.

Since I am not an expert in the area of property insurance, I highly recommend that anyone attempting to do "subject to" mortgage deals consult with their insurance agent. There are the risks of insurance challenges when doing "subject to" mortgage transactions.

Doctrine of Implied Assumption

When we buy any property ("subject to" mortgage or not), we take our financial commitments to lenders very seriously. We treat "subject to" mortgages and pay on them as seriously as if they were our own.

Unfortunately, not everyone who engages in "subject to" mortgage transactions does so. To make matters worse, there seems to a prevailing belief in certain circles that if you buy a "subject to" mortgage and the deal somehow goes bad, there is very little risk to you.

> *"There seems to a prevailing belief in certain circles that if you buy a 'subject to' mortgage and the deal somehow goes bad, there is very little risk to you."*

Of course, how widespread this belief is depends on the state or community in which you work, but I will say that I do not entirely agree with this belief. There is the matter of personal and business reputation if you work in a smaller city community as we do. But there is also a legal risk.

According to James Karp's and Elliot Klayman's textbook, *Real Estate Law*, 5th Edition, a number of states have extended responsibility to the buyer if the buyer engages in a "subject to" mortgage transaction under the Doctrine of Implied Assumption.

Under this Doctrine, although we have not formally assumed the loan, by virtue of having the property in our name, taking over the loan payments, and profiting from it, we are considered, as buyers, to have assumed the terms of the loan and could suffer liability if something were to go wrong.

> *"We may not have formally assumed the loan, but what we do can very well fall with the realm of implied assumption."*

Of course, this assumption would have to be proven in a court of law, but nevertheless the risk exists for anyone who chooses to buy a property with a "subject to" mortgage. We may not have formally assumed the loan, but what we do can very well fall within the realm of implied assumption.

Naturally, you should consult your local real estate attorney in such matters if you are truly curious about this issue.

However, we take a conservative approach. We simply assume that once we buy someone's property with a "subject to" mortgage, we are on the hook for the loan and the responsibility fully lies with us. This thought is a great motivator for us to enter into only profitable deals and to continue to be financially responsible.

"Due-on-Sale" Clause

When it comes to doing "subject to" mortgage transactions, there is perhaps no other topic more hotly discussed and debated than the infamous "due-on-sale" clause.

Quite simply, the "due-on-sale" clause is the wording contained in most modern mortgages which allows a lender to call a loan due in the event of a "sale" or other qualifying transaction.

> *"A violation of a 'due-on-sale' clause is not a criminal offense."*

Because the discussion of the "due-on-sale" clause, its history, and the surrounding issues is an entire subject of its own, I will only address it in the context of doing a "subject to" mortgage.

For newcomers, there are generally two issues surrounding "due-on-sale" clauses to consider: the legal issue and the ethical issue.

First, a violation of a "due-on-sale" clause is not a criminal offense. As Attorney Bill Bronchick says in his lectures, "There is no 'due-on-sale' jail." You will not be arrested by a law enforcement officer simply because you took over someone's loan. However, you could get in serious legal trouble if you willfully and intentionally took over someone else's loan and intentionally and willfully defaulted on the loan.

Remember, a "subject to" mortgage occurs only when legal title is transferred while the underlying loan remains in the original buyer's name. The risk of due-on-sale only occurs once the title is transferred.

When we buy a property with a "subject to" mortgage, we have two disclosure issues facing us – one to the lender and one to the seller.

What does a "Due-on-Sale" Clause Look Like?

Contrary to popular belief, there is no such monster in any mortgage document that points to itself with a specific name or label, "due-on-sale clause".

The infamous "due-on-sale clause" is often the paragraph that discusses "acceleration of the loan."

This is one "due-on-sale" clause from an Alabama mortgage.

Transfer of the Property or a Beneficial Interest in Borrower. *If all or any part of the Property or any interest in it is sold or transferred (or if a beneficial interest in Borrower is sold or transferred and Borrower is not a natural person) without Lender's prior written consent, Lender may, at its option, require immediate payment in full of all sums secured by this Security Instrument. However, this option shall not be exercised by Lender if exercise is prohibited by federal law as of the date of this Security Instrument.*

If Lender exercises this option, Lender shall give Borrower notice of acceleration. The notice shall provide a period of not less than 30 days form the date the notice is delivered or mailed within which Borrower must pay all sums secured by this Security Instrument. If Borrower fails to pay these sums prior to the expiration of this period, Lender may invoke any remedies permitted by this Security Instrument without further notice or demand on Borrower.

This is one "due-on-sale" clause from a Georgia Security Deed (mortgage).

Sale Without Credit Approval. *Lender shall, if permitted by applicable law (including Section 341(d) of the Garn-St. Germain Depository Institutions Act of 1982, 12 U.S.C. 1701j-3(d)) and with the prior approval of the Secretary, require immediate payment in full of all sums secured by this Security Instrument if:*

(i) All or part of the Property, or a beneficial interest in a trust owning all or part of the Property, is sold or otherwise transferred (other than by devise or descent), and

(ii) The Property is not occupied by the purchaser or grantee as his or her principal residence, or the purchaser or grantee does so occupy the Property but his or her credit has not been approved in accordance with the requirements of the Secretary.

Seller Disclosure

Because most of our sellers are unfamiliar with many of the subtleties of titles and mortgages, we educate our sellers in layman's terms about what we are doing. We tell our sellers that we will be transferring title to our company but will be keeping the existing loan in place. When that occurs, we will begin managing the property and maintaining the loan on their behalf.

We tell them that in order for us to complete the deal, there are documents they must sign. These documents include a Limited Power of Attorney, a new Warranty Deed, and other supporting documents which grant us "permission" to take over the property and manage it.

As part of the disclosure process, we also tell them the risks of the "due-on-sale" clause. When title transfers, there is a possibility that the lender could immediately call the loan due. And if that were to happen and the problem were not remedied, the lender could take legal steps to initiate the foreclosure process on the grounds of a "due-on-sale" violation.

Once we say that, we also quickly follow up by making some important points. Most lenders will not enforce "due-on-sale" for the following reasons:

- Most lenders do not want the property. They simply want continued loan payments. Lenders want as much as possible to stay away from the property. Lenders foreclose on a property only as a last resort to protect their financial interests.
- Most lenders will not intentionally ruin the borrower's credit by foreclosing on a property where the loan is current and performing. They do not need the negative publicity that goes with the territory of forcing a "good loan" to "go bad".
- It is both expensive and time-consuming to initiate and complete the foreclosure process.

Generally, most sellers find the points we make to be compelling enough to go ahead with the transaction once we give them assurances that we are able to meet the financial obligations.

But What if the Lender Calls the Loan Due Anyway?

We know the likelihood of a loan being called due is actually very small, provided the property is maintained, the loan is current, and property insurance is current.

However, in the unlikely event that a loan is called due, we tell the seller that we would take care of such an event by:

- Formally assuming the loan.
- Refinancing the property with another lender.

Why We Don't Worry About "Due-On-Sale"

There are many reasons why we are not overly concerned with due on sale. It does not mean we are unaware or do not care. ***Our confidence comes from our knowledge and ability to deal with it if it does occur.***

"Our confidence comes from our knowledge and ability to deal with it if it does occur."

Most institutional lenders have a department devoted to properties they own through foreclosure actions. Those foreclosed properties are generally known by lenders as "real estate owned" or REOs. Most of these lenders try their best to minimize REOs. It is not in most lenders' best interest to intentionally cause a REO.

That is why we continually emphasize the importance of making continued payments and having the ability to financially cover those payments when vacancies occur. Lenders are generally happy if payments are made and the loan is current.

"We Don't Care Where the Money Comes From"

When I first started out doing "subject to" mortgage transactions, one of the things I quickly wanted to find out was to separate the theory of a lender's invoking the due-on-sale provision and the practicality of their enforcing it.

> *"Lenders are generally happy if payments are made and the loan is current."*

When I called lenders to fax in the Power of Attorney (POA) our sellers signed for us, I discovered it was actually a common occurrence for lenders to receive documents with instructions to give third-parties access and control over the account.

Lenders are very accustomed to third-parties such as property managers, attorneys, accountants, insurance agents, and other professionals accessing loan information. They are also used to receiving instructions for address changes, statements, coupon books, and insurance changes.

And when there is an arrearage on a loan, the Collections Department (sometimes called Loss Mitigaion) is often gratified that someone is calling for instructions to reinstate the loan.

I have found that once you provide the necessary written authorization by the borrower, such as a signed and notarized POA, lenders are often more than happy to deal with you. They are happy to cooperate in making address changes, getting you coupon books, and providing current loan information as long as it is in the spirit of servicing the loan.

> *"We will not issue funds to reinstate the loan unless our financial interests are protected."*

When we deal with sellers to buy with a "subject to" mortgage, they sometimes enter the early stages of foreclosure. The lender is no longer handling the account and it has been transferred to a real estate attorney.

In many of those conversations, I often speak to the attorney or the clerk handling the account and ask them if they have any problems with us (a third-party) reinstating the loan. Sometimes they will ask why we would reinstate the loan. I tell them directly that we are a property management company that has been contacted by the borrower to negotiate on their behalf and perhaps to reinstate the loan.

However, we will not issue funds to reinstate the loan unless our financial interests are protected.

I then ask: "Do you or the lender have any problems that the borrower and I have an agreement whereby I have a financial interest in reinstating the loan?"

You know what they say? No problem. They say it makes sense that we would have an agreement with the borrower to have a financial interest if we are the ones issuing funds on their behalf to reinstate the loan.

> *"When I am on the phone with either the lender or the attorney, I try as much as I can to take a human approach."*

In fact, nearly everyone I spoke to in each case did not care. To paraphrase their response, "nothing would make us happier than to receive the money to reinstate the loan and to stop the foreclosure." They don't care who pays or who the party is so long as they receive certified funds.

When I am on the phone with either the lender or the attorney, I try as much as I can to take a human approach. I position myself as the outside third-party being called in by the borrower because I have the expertise and the funds to solve the problem.

In all cases, I make it understood that I am not doing this as a "favor" to the borrower. I am doing it because it is my job and that I have a financial interest in profiting from this transaction. The lender and the attorney easily accept my position. In their minds, no company would reinstate the loan unless they could profit from it. They never ask the nature of the transaction, and I do not give them specifics of the "subject to" mortgage transaction I intend to complete.

The foreclosure attorney represents the lender at this late stage. They simply want the money, and they don't care who pays it or where the money comes from.

This is evidenced each month when lenders accept our checks month after month, and it is clear that the borrower is not making the payments.

Anecdotal Evidence

Many of my investor friends also do "subject to" mortgage deals. They are located throughout the U.S. As a sampling, I have an estimated 200 "subject to" mortgage deals to draw from as I write this.

> *"It is damn good evidence compared to cynics and skeptics who have no experience and nothing good to say about 'subject to' mortgages."*

I am happy to say in my discussions with other investors that they corroborate my own experience that lenders are more than happy to receive payments, and it doesn't matter who writes the checks.

Scientifically speaking, 200 out of several thousands of these types of transactions is not a true representative sampling. But for me, it is damn good evidence compared to cynics and skeptics who have no experience and nothing good to say about "subject to" mortgages.

Attorney opinions

My real estate attorney and I have discussed the "due-on-sale" issue, and her answer is very short regarding most concerns over due-on-sale. You are generally safe as long as you keep paying lenders. They only want the money.

> *"My real estate attorney and I have discussed the due-on-sale issue, and her answer is very short regarding most concerns over due-on-sale."*

In the unlikely circumstance that a loan is called, she happens to agree with me that the appropriate action is for us to either formally assume the loan or to find someone to refinance the property.

In Bill Bronchick's course on "Alternative Real Estate Financing," he provides some great supplementary material in the discussion of "due-on-sale" issues.

Original Purpose of "Due-on-Sale" Clause

In *Real Estate Finance Law*, the authors Nelson & Whitman state that "while the clause is sometimes used to protect mortgagees against transfers that endanger mortgage security or increase the risk of default, its major purpose is to enable mortgagees to force the repayment of lower-than-market interest rate loans during periods of rising interest rates."

In the passage quoted, the authors clearly imply that the threat of acceleration is often used as a way to compel the transferee to pay a higher interest rate. Interestingly, even under these circumstances, the lender still does not want the property back.

> *"The threat of acceleration is often used as a way to compel the transferee to pay a higher interest rate."*

What is worse than holding a low-interest loan is holding a loan that suddenly does not perform and simultaneously harms the old borrower's credit and account.

In our current economic climate and in the near future, it doesn't seem likely that lenders will enforce the "due-on-sale" clause based on interest rates. In fact, as of this writing, most of the loans we pay on actually have higher interest rates than the rates being offered today!

Summary

There are always risks to every investment. It is no different when buying property with a "subject to" mortgage. And there are several areas of risk to consider. Evaluating the overall risk often involves ensuring the "subject to" mortgage financing remains intact for years to come, not to have it unravel due to lender or seller issues. Perhaps no issue is of greater concern and hotly debated than the "due-on-sale" issue. However, what it really comes down to, for us, is that we create peace of mind for ourselves by having the confidence in our abilities to deal with that and the other risks surrounding any "subject to" mortgage transaction.

CHAPTER

7

Due Diligence

Once our offer is accepted by the seller and a purchase and sales contract is signed, we move into the due diligence phase. "Due diligence" is a legal term that means a process of doing all essential research to determine whether the deal is a good one before proceeding with the transaction.

As with any investment property purchase, there is a series of steps for the due diligence process which we follow. Some steps are those we would take for any kind of property, regardless of the finance method. Other steps are specific to "subject to" mortgage transactions.

The due diligence steps for a "subject to" mortgage transaction from beginning to end are:

- Property Inspection
- Investment Returns & Profitability (The Numbers)
- Seller
- Release of Information
- Lender
- Loan Status
- Foreclosure Attorney
- Title check
- Insurance

Lease-Option Criteria

The due diligence we primarily do for a property is one we would perform to sell with a lease-option. The only reason we evaluate under lease-option criteria is simply because it is our specialty. We like to buy a solid investment property and then lease-option it to a tenant-buyer for a profit.

> *"We determine FMV by our standards, not necessarily what others, including real estate professionals, say the property is worth."*

The specific steps for doing due diligence on a property are largely dependent on how we intend to profit from the property. Our due diligence (which is property specific) for a "subject to" mortgage transaction is based on our standard that we will never take on a property in which we cannot carry the vacancy and still make the monthly payments. We will also not buy a property where the FMV (Fair Market Value) is less than the loan balance. (Again, we determine FMV by our standards, not necessarily what others, including real estate professionals, say the property is worth.)

We work in a market where there is low appreciation, so buying a property at market value is the maximum risk we will take on. When we buy a property with little or no equity, we clearly cannot renovate and resell the property conventionally. There is simply no room for profit. The only way to potentially profit is simply to rent or lease-option the property for a monthly payment spread.

Property Inspection

We conduct a property inspection on every property we buy. Many of the items we list here are also included in a previous book, *TurnKey Investing with Lease-Options.*

Typically, we look at the following items:

Electrical panel - Does it use circuit breakers or fuses? Although we clearly prefer circuit breakers, we will occasionally buy houses that use the old-style fuse boxes.

Environmental units - We look to see if the house has a functional central air-conditioning unit. If not, does the house have sufficient window air-conditioning units? We prefer central heating; however, many of the older houses we buy require gas to produce the heat. For us, the best possible scenario is to have electrical heating.

Water Heater - We look to see if it requires gas or electric to operate. We much prefer electrical water heaters to gas water heaters.

Roof – We look to see if the roof is in reasonably good condition and verify this by walking through the interior while looking at the ceiling for indications of any water leaks.

Interior walls – Primarily, we look to see if there is damage or if there are any holes in the walls. Secondarily, we want to see if the general appearance is acceptable or whether the walls clearly need repainting.

Carpeting and flooring – The majority of homes we look at and buy have carpeting. We inspect the carpet to ascertain whether it is salvageable or whether it will clearly need to be replaced. We look at the flooring in the bathroom and kitchen for moisture damage.

Plumbing – We inspect bathroom and kitchen faucets for any leaks and check to see if the toilets flush properly.

Doors and locks – We inspect the doors, locks, and doorframes leading to the exterior. We place a lesser priority on locks for bedrooms, bathrooms, and other interior doors.

Windows – We inspect for damaged or broken windows that would expose the interior to the outside weather.

Landscaping – We look to see if the lawn needs to be cut or any shrubs or bushes need to be trimmed. We also look to see if there is any debris or trash in the yard area that might diminish the curb appeal of the property.

Interior Trash and debris – We inspect the interior of the property for any remaining personal contents, trash, or debris left by the seller.

Appliances – We inspect the kitchen appliances (if any) to ensure they are operational.

Although it is not our specialty, we occasionally buy property that clearly needs renovation work. Under these circumstances, we make sure there is enough potential equity we can create and profit from before buying the house. Our cash flow is often very thin, but the upside equity potential is sometimes too good to pass up.

Keep in mind that a "subject to" mortgage is simply a tool to finance a property purchase. The property-specific due diligence we do can vary from property to property. The reason it is different is that the way we plan to profit influences the way we conduct the property specific portion of the due diligence.

> *"The property-specific due diligence we do can vary from property to property."*

Investment Returns & Profitability (The Numbers)

With any property investment, regardless of the type of financing we use, we always calculate the likely returns we will make. After all, with any investment, it really comes down to the numbers.

Regardless of how much a seller wants to sell us their property, if we cannot see a reasonable rate of return or good equity potential, there is no point in acquiring the property even though the seller is willing to let us take over the property with a "subject to" mortgage.

Often, we will make a preliminary estimate concerning whether a property is even worth looking at during the initial call from the seller. By this stage, we are simply reconfirming that we will in fact make a good return if we consummate the transaction.

As you view our sample analysis, bear in mind we use conservative numbers. Actual values and numbers can vary greatly from property-to-property and seller-to-seller.

As with many investments, we also base some of our decisions on the locale, local economics and trends, and other intangible elements that are not always reflected in a financial analysis.

Profitability Analysis: Lease-Option

	FMV: $80,000	Market Rents: $795 / mo.
1st Mtg:	$62,000	$500 / mo.
2nd Mtg:	$13,000	$100 / mo.
Profit:	$ 5,000 Equity 93.8% FMV "Little equity"	$195 / mo. cash flow x 12 months $2,340 annually
Arrearage:	$ 1,900	
Vacancy:	$ 1,800 (3-mo.)	
Marketing:	$ 450 (3-mo.)	
Total Cash Investment:	$ 4,150	Cash-on-cash Returns: 56.4%

Seller

It may seem odd that I have included the seller as part of the due diligence process. Nevertheless, it is a very important part of making a "subject to" mortgage transaction work. The seller has to be completely onboard with the concept and fully accept both the advantages and disadvantages of completing the transaction.

> *"The seller has to be completely onboard with the concept and fully accept both the advantages and disadvantages of completing the transaction."*

There are enough challenges in dealing with an investment property and making it perform well without having the seller potentially jeopardize the integrity of the financing.

Naturally, we would never schedule a closing if we had earlier detected reluctance from the seller. They have to be both *comfortable and cooperative* during, and even after, the closing.

Some of the questions we ask the seller are:

- Do you understand that the loan will continue to be in your name and continue to be on your credit report?
- Do you understand that we do not know when the loan will be fully paid off and satisfied?

- Are you sure you would not like to sell the property yourself or have a real estate agent sell your property?
- Are you sure you would not like more time to think about this?
- Have you and your spouse fully discussed this?
- Are you sure you would like to move forward and complete the paperwork?
- Would you like to be relieved of the house and the payments?

The questions have been paraphrased for the sake of this handbook. We phrase the questions in a way that will encourage a positive response from our seller. If we have negotiated properly, the seller will conclude that what we are proposing is ultimately the best solution for them.

> *"We phrase questions in a way that will encourage a positive response from our seller."*

Often, it comes down to the fact that they no longer have the time to wait for a conventional sale. Any more delays will result in further inconvenience, additional responsibility, and great financial difficulties.

Admittedly, dealing with sellers requires a good intuitive sense of where they are psychologically, emotionally, and financially. There is no one specific way we deal with sellers except that we want to make sure they are fully committed to the transaction.

Release of Information Authorization

Before we can get information and verify the status of the loan, we get an authorized Release of Information Form signed by the seller. There are privacy laws that protect the borrower from unwanted inquiries into their financial matters, and lenders are very strict in enforcing the rules.

Frequently, we attempt to get loan information through an automated telephone service where all that is required is the loan account number and the seller's Social Security number.

Unfortunately, this only works if the loan is current. We sometimes have to speak to a customer service representative to find out the reinstatement amount if the loan has fallen into arrears, or if the account has been assigned to a foreclosure attorney. The only way they will speak with us is if we fax in a Release of Information Authorization.

> *"There are privacy laws that protect the borrower from unwanted inquiries into their financial matters, and lenders are very strict in enforcing the rules."*

Alternatively, we get a Limited Power of Attorney instead of a Release of Information Authorization from the seller if we feel certain that we will likely buy this property based on preliminary information.

Lender

Having dealt with dozens of lenders, we have discovered that each lender has its own style of servicing the loan. In other words, customer service for loans varies somewhat from lender to lender especially when dealing with third parties (parties authorized by the borrower).

What we are evaluating during our call to the lender is how capable and how receptive the lender is to working with authorized third-parties, especially if the seller moves out of the property.

> *"What we are evaluating during our call to the lender is how capable and how receptive the lender is to working with authorized third-parties."*

After all, if we take over the seller's loan, we have to be able to interact easily with the lender regarding getting loan information, verifying payments, address changes, and ordering statements or payment books.

Typically, having a faxed Limited Power of Attorney on record with the lender is sufficient. However, we still encounter the occasional challenge of getting the cooperation we need. Usually, we get resistance from government-related agencies which provided special financing to our sellers.

I remember one particular instance when we chose not to buy a property with a "subject to" mortgage. We walked away from it even though the deal had profit potential and the seller was willing to work with us. Unfortunately, that government agency made it absolutely clear to us that if the seller were to move out of their property before their obligatory term, the agency would swiftly move to foreclose on the property even if payments were being made.

When that was told to us in no uncertain terms by the lender, we felt we had no choice but to let that particular deal go. It was simply too risky to take on the lender who was intent on foreclosing on the property.

> *"Most lenders are experienced with third-parties and are generally cooperative."*

Fortunately, most lenders are experienced with third-parties and are generally cooperative. But all it takes is one uncooperative lender to make our lives difficult, so we always make sure we check out the lender.

Loan Status

The time period between when the seller first contacts us and the time that the due diligence is being done (shortly before the scheduled closing), several weeks could have elapsed. A loan that is current can fall into arrears. Or a loan that is in mild arrears with the lender can suddenly be transferred to a foreclosure attorney.

When either one of these situations occur, a borderline deal can suddenly become a terrible deal. In fact, it can become a downright loser we may ultimately have to walk away from.

When we call the lender for a loan balance, we also look to see whether the status of the loan has changed significantly. Is the loan still being managed by the lender? If so, is the loan current or in arrears? If the loan is now in arrears, has it gotten worse? Has it gone to the foreclosure attorney? Can the deal still be profitable for us?

> *"A borderline deal can suddenly become a terrible deal."*

If we discover that the loan has changed for the worse and a borderline deal becomes an unsalvageable one, it is at this point we walk away.

In more serious situations where the lender has assigned the account to a foreclosure attorney and foreclosure is imminent, we have to quickly assess what it will take to reinstate the account. Often this means that we have to negotiate with the law firm handling the account to find out the least amount of money they are willing to take to stop foreclosure proceedings and where we have to send certified funds to stop the foreclosure.

It is during this phase that we get full authorization to ask the lender whatever questions we need answered.

Foreclosure Attorney

Occasionally, we buy properties that are in extreme arrears (four to six months), and the lender has assigned the loan to a foreclosure attorney. When that happens, foreclosure is imminent, usually within three weeks or less. We want to find out if we can stop foreclosure proceedings in time. And if so, how much will it cost us to do so? Will the investment be worthwhile for us?

> *"The challenge of buying a property with a 'subject to' mortgage, while the loan is being handled by the foreclosure attorney, is in reaching the correct person who can come up with accurate reinstatement fees."*

The challenge of buying a property with a "subject to" mortgage while the loan is being handled by the foreclosure attorney is in reaching the correct person who can come up with accurate reinstatement fees. We also have to be able to send funds quickly enough to stop foreclosure proceedings. Simultaneously, we try to negotiate down any fees that may have been added to the loan arrearage.

We have reinstated loans based on figures given to us by foreclosure attorneys. Unfortunately, in our experience, they almost never get it right despite our best efforts to get a definitive figure during the due diligence phase. We only find this out after we have bought the property, gained possession of the property, and sent in the monies needed to reinstate the loan.

Prior to reinstating the loan, we can technically back out of the deal at anytime. Unfortunately, once we reinstate the loan with certified funds of several thousand dollars, we no longer have the option of backing out. We are fully and financially committed to the deal at that point.

We now mentally add an additional $500.00 to any figure the foreclosure attorney gives us (and we hold that in reserves) since we occasionally seem to get these extra "surprises" after taking over the property.

Title Check

As with any other investment property purchase, we consider it mandatory to run a title check. We always ask the seller if they are aware of any liens on the property. Nearly always, the seller will say there are no liens on the property. Unfortunately, we occasionally discover there is in fact a lien or two on the property. We have found court judgments and liens that were attached to properties.

When that occurs, we make efforts to work with the seller to having the lien removed. If that cannot easily happen, we have to decide whether we are willing to take over the property and accept the lien.

Insurance

There are two parts to this due diligence check. Sometimes, the seller lets property insurance coverage lapse. In this case, lender-placed insurance is used to protect the lender's interest on the property. Unfortunately, lender-placed insurance is very expensive and can affect the deal.

In rural areas, getting property insurance at any price is sometimes an issue, so lender-placed insurance becomes the only option.

> *"We consider it mandatory to run a title check."*

Every property we purchase with a "subject to" mortgage ultimately starts with a homeowner's policy. Once the seller sells the property to us, we have to convert that policy into a landlord policy which is often more expensive than a homeowner's policy.

During the due diligence stage, we want to find out if there are any attributes of the property that will substantially increase the cost of property insurance. If so, a borderline deal can suddenly become an unprofitable one especially if we are looking to earn positive cash flow.

Summary

The due diligence phase is the final phase before proceeding to closing. If there is any fact-finding or fact-checking that must occur, it must happen at this time before it is too late. We must secure authorization from the seller to do a complete due diligence. Often, we incorporate due diligence steps prior to reaching this point. By doing this, it allows us to either discard the deal or move quickly into the closing phase.

CHAPTER

8

Closing the Deal

If we have done a good job of evaluating the seller, creating a rapport with him, and have done our due diligence properly, it should be a relatively quick and easy matter to do the closing. A "subject to" mortgage closing is far easier and quicker than a conventional financing closing.

We schedule a "subject to" mortgage transaction closing like any other closing. We want our real estate attorney to conduct the closing for us.

In a closing, conveyance of title occurs. In simpler terms, ownership is transferred. Both buyer and seller come together to sign pre-prepared contracts and agreements necessary for smooth transfer of ownership and possession.

Closing Attorney

In our area, it is customary to have real estate closings performed by a real estate attorney. In other areas of the U.S., title companies perform the same function. We treat our "subject to" mortgage transactions as professionally as we do closings with conventional financing.

Simply put, having a professional third-party close our "subject to" mortgage transactions gives our transaction a high degree of credibility and legitimacy. The closing attorney (or title company) prepares the contracts and agreements and has the seller sign the documents. We simply show up to inspect the documents and meet with the seller. By doing the closing this way, we lessen the opportunity for the seller to later challenge the transaction for any reason.

Title Insurance

There are generally two schools of thought regarding the issue of getting title insurance for "subject to" mortgage transactions.

Some say that title insurance is an unnecessary expense especially if the loan being taken over is reasonably "new" (less than three years). The rationale is that a full title check was done and title insurance was bought when the seller initially bought the property. The idea is that the title is "solid" up to that point. The risk we incur is that hidden liens can appear and attach to the property between the time the seller bought the property with conventional financing and the time we bought the property with a "subject to" mortgage.

"Arguments by opponents of title insurance are that the benefits and need for title insurance is often oversold and exaggerated."

Additional arguments by opponents of title insurance are that the benefits and need for title insurance is often oversold and exaggerated; that there is enough fine print in any policy for an insurance company to get out of paying if there are significant problems.

Although we do a title check to uncover liens or title problems, it is certainly not a flawless process, so the possibility always exists that we may not have clear title.

Conservative investors prefer to get title insurance for each and every transaction they do. They view it as a cost of doing business to eliminate any risk of title problems.

Personally, I think title insurance has its place in certain circumstances. I take a slightly more liberal approach. I am not inclined to buy title insurance for newer loans because I believe it is highly unlikely a newer loan will experience a title problem. I am more inclined to buy title insurance for older loans where there is a greater likelihood of a title problem.

> *"You bear the responsibility of consulting with an advisor best suited to your situation."*

However, let me warn you that we are not professional advisors here. We are private investors who primarily invest for ourselves. The business of investing involves determining what risk we are willing to take. As such, we bear the responsibility of our decisions.

Here, I simply share my opinions. As a reader, you bear the responsibility of consulting with an advisor best suited to your situation. Regarding my "official" position on title insurance, if you are at all concerned, I would simply play it safe, get peace of mind, and buy title insurance for your "subject to" mortgage transactions. However, I would be hypocritical if I did not disclose that we often do not obtain title insurance due to the nature of the deals that we close.

Types of Closings

There are three ways to conduct "subject to" mortgage transaction closings. There are bank closings, "kitchen table" closings, and customary closings.

Bank Closings – Our Early Days

Earlier, I wrote about how we do all our real estate closings with our real estate attorney. This is true today. However, before we discovered that our real estate attorney was also knowledgeable about "subject to" mortgage transactions, we performed our own closings at the bank, not at the real estate attorney's office.

"Technically, a 'subject to' mortgage transaction closing can occur anywhere as long as there is a notary public available to notarize documents."

Technically, a "subject to" mortgage transaction closing can occur anywhere as long as there is a notary public available to notarize documents. However, in my effort to legitimize my transactions, I did the next best thing to closing with a real estate attorney. I chose to do closings at our local bank.

I bring this up because some of you may not be able to immediately find a title company or real estate attorney to do your closings. As a temporary stop-gap measure, closing at the local bank was the next best thing for us. However, keep in mind the local bank can only provide office space and notary services, nothing more. They cannot prepare forms or deeds. They also cannot advise anyone in real estate matters.

"Kitchen Table" Closings

I have included this section to give my opinion on what is sometimes taught by some seminar instructors on how to conduct "subject to" mortgage transaction closings. Some teach that you can and should do "kitchen table" closings.

What they mean by a "kitchen table" closing is that you must first prepare all the forms and documents at home ahead of time. You then contact a notary public and arrange to have him meet you at the seller's home and have them sign the paperwork in their house!

> *While a 'kitchen table' closing is technically legal and allowed, I view it as low in credibility and professionalism."*

And while a "kitchen table" closing is technically legal and allowed, I view it as low in credibility and professionalism. I think it lends itself to too many problems down the road if the seller decides to challenge the deal.

As I mentioned throughout this book, it is incredibly important that the seller feels good and takes seriously the "subject to" mortgage transaction. Having their ongoing cooperation throughout the next several years by making the transaction credible is essential for having a long-lived "subject to" mortgage continue to work for you.

Making the "subject to" mortgage closing as close as possible to a customary closing with conventional financing goes a long way to communicating the message. The sellers leave with a closing packet clearly documenting who did the closing and how it was done with their copies of the paperwork.

> *"It can only lead to potential trouble and conflict with the sellers years later if they ever choose to contest the transaction."*

Conducting a "kitchen table" closing in someone's messy home, no matter how well prepared ahead of time, leaves an unprofessional and "unofficial" atmosphere that I do not want sellers to have. It can only lead to potential trouble and conflict with the sellers years later if they ever choose to contest the transaction.

Customary Closings

I classify the closings we do with our real estate attorney as a "customary closing" because it is customary to the area we are in. In other parts of the U.S., it is customary to have title companies, or even lenders do closings.

I am a firm proponent of performing customary closings with "subject to" mortgage transactions for credibility and perception purposes.

Land Trusts

A land trust is a legal device that allows a property owner to legally hold property without being on title. This is accomplished by establishing a trust (through a set of documents) whereby a trustee is selected, empowered, and entrusted (often by the beneficiary) to handle, manage, convey, and perform other actions pertaining to the property.

Simply, a trustee is *entrusted* with responsibilities and ensures that the beneficiary receives the practical benefits of the arrangement. In essence, the beneficiary could be considered the "true owner." The trustee serves as the "front manager" for the beneficiary.

> *"I do like the design and idea of land trusts."*

The land trust I discuss in this section originated in Illinois where using land trusts is a fairly common practice to hold property. In other parts of the U.S., the land trust is less popular and almost obscure in some areas.

It often comes down to the progressiveness, sophistication, and customs of the local area.

To begin with, I do like the design and idea of land trusts. They are relatively easy to implement and do allow us some anonymity as to the true "owners" of the property. This anonymity happens because only the trustee shows up in public records, not the beneficiary. The document that names the beneficiary is an unrecorded document.

Although considered a legal entity that "shields" the beneficiary, land trusts in themselves do not provide the same asset protection or the tax advantages as corporations, limited partnerships, or limited liability corporations (LLCs). Land trusts are considered "flow through" entities. Both benefits and liabilities ultimately fall to the beneficiary, the "true" owner of the property.

To get the asset protection and tax advantages with the land trust, you would have to also create a corporation, limited partnership, or limited liability corporation (LLC), and make that entity the beneficiary.

"The discussion of using land trusts with a 'subject to' mortgage often revolves around minimizing the risk of having a lender enforce the 'due-on-sale' clause."

Please note that the use of corporate entities and land trusts with real estate and the tax consequences are beyond the scope of this book.

While using land trusts to hold property is a good idea in general, the discussion of using land trusts with a "subject to" mortgage often revolves around minimizing the risk of having a lender enforce the "due-on-sale" clause.

How this occurs is that the land trust is set up with the appearance that the original borrower is still the beneficiary. And when done correctly, that situation is true. However, the true "sale" of the property occurs when the original borrower assigns their beneficial interest to the buyer. If we are the buyers, we become the new beneficiaries of the land trust.

This assignment (transfer) of beneficial interest is a legal but unrecorded event in terms of public records.

While a somewhat effective strategy on paper, it is not fool-proof. The transfer is still a violation of the due-on-sale clause, and the risk is still very real. However, the lender would have to "prove" the violation by going through the extra step of verifying who the beneficiary would be.

> *"Many insurance companies have difficulties understanding the land trust."*

Additionally, many insurance companies have difficulties understanding the land trust. Depending on how the property insurance policy is written, the lender, if it chooses, could scrutinize and discover that the beneficiary has indeed been transferred away from the original borrower.

As a practical matter, most institutional lenders have thousands of accounts to monitor for the basics.

- Is the account current?
- Is the mailing address current?
- Is the property adequately insured?
- Are their interests protected as the first mortgagor?

If the answers to these questions are "yes", there is generally little reason for the lender to be alarmed.

They have way too many accounts to deal with where the answer to one or more of the questions is "no."

I would like to re-emphasize that you do not have to use a land trust to do a "subject to" mortgage transaction. It could be as simple as having a new warranty deed prepared and signed into your name as an individual.

Alternatively, the deed could be prepared and signed into the corporate entity of your choice. Or lastly, you have a deed prepared and have the seller sign it to the land trust with the trustee of your choice.

More Information on Land Trusts

The subject of land trusts, its intricacies, and usage is an entire subject of its own. There are entire publications and courses devoted to it.

I recommend the following publications and resources for people who want to learn more about land trusts. These publications also come with baseline forms you can use. Personally, we use the land trust documents written and designed by Colorado Attorney Bill Bronchick.

- *Land Trusts for Privacy & Profit* by Mark Warda
- *Land Trusts in Florida* by Mark Warda
- *Step-by-Step Guide to Land Trusts* by Bill Bronchick
- *Street Smart ASSET PROTECTION & ESTATE PLANNING - Land Trusts* by Louis Brown

Closing Documents

Our closing documents for a "subject to" mortgage transaction consist of the following:

- Limited Power of Attorney
- Warranty Deed to Trustee
- Trust Agreement
- Assignment of Beneficial Interest
- "Subject to" Mortgage Disclosure Letter
- Notice to Insurance Company
- HUD-1 Settlement Statement
- Seller's Forwarding Information
- Compliance Agreement

Finally, notarize and sign the documents, then get the keys if the sellers have already moved out.

Limited Power of Attorney

This document is a variation of the Power of Attorney. By signing this document, the seller grants us the authority to manage any or all affairs pertaining to the management of the property and the loan on their behalf. This document is property-specific and is designed to give us all-encompassing authority to fully transact business.

Warranty Deed to Trustee

This special warranty deed has specific clauses which grant the selected trustee specific powers to convey and manage property on behalf of the beneficiary.

This type of warranty deed is designed to work with a land trust, giving the beneficiary an extra layer of privacy and anonymity.

Trust Agreement

The trust agreement establishes the existence of a land trust, the trustee, and its beneficiaries. The trust agreement specifies the powers and responsibilities of the trustee to work on behalf of the beneficiary.

Assignment of Beneficial Interest

After the land trust is established and the trustee is appointed, an assignment of beneficial interest in effect transfers the ownership from the seller to us as the buyers. This transfer is an unrecorded but a very real event that gives us all the practical benefits of ownership.

"Subject to" Mortgage Disclosure Letter

This letter, in laymen's terms, discloses to the seller that completing this transaction may trigger the "due-on-sale" clause. It also says that we will not formally assume the loan into our names. We also disclose that this loan may remain in their name for an undetermined amount of time. However, we agree to continue make payments for the life of the loan.

Notice to Insurance Company

This letter informs the insurance company that we will be replacing the homeowners insurance with a landlord policy. Some insurance companies do not honor the Power of Attorney document and require this letter.

HUD-1 Settlement Statement

Details of the closing, the fees, and the outstanding loan amount are outlined in this document. Because this document is the nationwide standard for real estate closings within the U.S., having our seller sign off this document is incredibly important to protecting our interests should there be any future dispute of the validity of our transaction.

Seller's Forwarding Information

We get the seller's new contact information including their mailing address and telephone number for our records. We use this information to contact the seller in case there are any residual issues that come up.

Compliance Agreement

The seller agrees to sign any documents that might be missing to fully complete the transaction. We do not want to be held hostage because of one missing or forgotten document. The seller agrees to cooperate to fulfilling the legal details relating to the spirit of the sale.

Get the Keys

At the closing table, we prefer to get the keys before they leave. This presumes they have already moved out prior to the closing. And when we get the keys, it is understood we then have both legal and physical possession of the property.

Occasionally, the seller wants to or needs to stay at the property until the closing is completed. When this happens, we obviously do not get the keys at the closing table and we have to wait until after the closing before we can take physical possession.

> *"We make every effort to quickly get legal possession by encouraging the seller to move out as soon as possible."*

In these situations, we do tell them we cannot issue any payments until they move out and we get full possession of the property.

However, once closing is complete, we make every effort to quickly get legal possession by encouraging the seller to move out as soon as possible. Often, they move within a few days after closing.

As an incentive, we remind the seller if we do not make payments to the lender, it could further damage or jeopardize their account and credit. This is usually a good incentive for them to move out quickly especially if they care about their credit rating and most especially if they are headed into foreclosure.

We have legal possession of the property when the keys are handed to us and when the premises are vacated.

Summary

Perhaps no greater sense of satisfaction can be achieved than reaching and ultimately closing the deal. More specifically, having a closing come together smoothly for both the seller and ourselves coordinated by our closing attorney. A formal closing at our attorney's office is often an essential ceremonial gesture for the benefit of our seller to let them know that the "subject to" mortgage transaction they have signed is both a significant and fully lawful sales transaction that would be upheld in a court of law.

CHAPTER

9

After the Closing

After the closing, there is a series of tasks we must perform to complete the transfer. Although the closing transfers title to us, there are several housekeeping items we must take care of if we are to successfully manage the property and the loan.

Get Legal Possession of the Property

As I stated in the preceding chapter, we prefer to get the keys before they leave. *What follows is essentially a review. This has been provided for the benefit of the selective reader who wishes to only read about issues after the closing.*

Occasionally, the seller needs or wants to stay at the property until after the closing is completed. When this happens, we obviously do not get the keys at the closing table.

However, we make every effort to quickly get legal possession by encouraging the seller to move out as soon as possible. Often, they move within a few days after closing. As an incentive, we remind the sellers we cannot issue any payments to the lender until we have physical possession of the property. This is usually a good incentive for them to move out quickly especially if they care about their credit rating and most especially if they are headed into foreclosure.

We have legal possession of the property when the keys are handed to us and when the premises are vacated.

Foreclosure Attorney

Once we have possession of the property but know it faces impending foreclosure, we immediately contact the foreclosure attorney and quickly fax in our Power of Attorney if we haven't already done so earlier. We then immediately get the latest information, requirements, and instructions to reinstate the loan.

During the due diligence phase, most of the details and instructions for loan reinstatement should have already been communicated to us. Nevertheless, in case anything has changed we will reconfirm the amount of certified funds they require from us and the mailing address to which we will send a certified check.

Once we have that information, we make arrangements with our bank to have a cashier's check cut; then we send it via Federal Express overnight service.

"Once we have possession of the property but know it faces impending foreclosure, we immediately contact the foreclosure attorney and quickly fax in our Power of Attorney."

We also provide instructions to have any correspondence directed to our mailing address, not the seller's mailing address.

Within two days time, the attorney should have received the cashier's check, and the foreclosure will have been halted. As far as the foreclosure attorney is concerned, the loan is fully reinstated. However, it will usually be several days before the reinstatement process comes to a conclusion, and the account is once again handled by the lender.

A loan that would have gone into foreclosure and ruined the seller's credit to become another statistic is saved by our doing a "subject to" mortgage transaction.

Lender

Once the impending foreclosure has been ended through our reinstatement funds, we move to communicate with the lender. Of course, if there were no impending foreclosure situation, the lender would be the first party we would contact after taking possession of the property.

We quickly fax in our Power of Attorney and our mailing address change request so that we have the authority to actively manage the loan account. Lenders generally tell us we have to wait at least 24 hours before the documents are recorded into their system.

"Once the impending foreclosure has been ended through our restatement funds, we move to communicate with the lender."

However, for some peculiar reason, it seems we generally have to fax in our documents twice before it sticks. We generally have to do so when we follow up, and they tell us they still do not have the documents when a few days have already passed.

We order the necessary coupon book or have the monthly statements redirected to us as appropriate.

If the loan was in arrears but not with the foreclosure attorney, we get instructions from the lender to bring the loan account current. If the arrearage is on the verge of going to a foreclosure attorney, the lender will generally insist on certified funds or a cashier's check and have it sent via overnight mail.

However, if the arrearage is mild and there is a lower level of urgency, we simply issue our company check and mail it in like any other payment.

Property Preparation

Regarding the property itself, once the seller has moved out and we are given the keys, we take possession of the property and immediately begin to have the property prepared for resale. Typically, we do this simultaneously as we are dealing with the lender.

When the property is in our possession, we quickly move on as many fronts as possible. Property preparation is an important stage that we start as quickly as possible to make the property a profitable investment for us.

> *"Property preparation is an important stage that we start as quickly as possible to make the property a profitable investment for us."*

In our case, we generally prepare our properties for resale with "owner-financing" using our TurnKey Lease-Options Management System.

We activate water and electric service so we can do a thorough inspection after the seller moves out. It also allows our hired help to begin working on our property.

> *"We generally prepare our properties for resale with 'owner-financing' using our TurnKey Lease-Options Management System."*

Some of the things we do to prepare the property for resale include hiring a yard-care person to clear the yard of trash, mow the lawn, and trim bushes and shrubbery. We also hire a housekeeper to clean and wipe down all surfaces as well as mop and vacuum the floors. We may also make minor repairs to leaky toilets, faucets, air-conditioning units, and appliances. We may also re-key the property.

The details of what we do to prepare our properties for resale on a lease-option is beyond the scope of this book and more thoroughly discussed in my previous book, *TurnKey Investing with Lease-Options*.

Other Methods of Profit

Keep in mind as a concept that a "subject to" mortgage transaction is primarily a method of buying and financing the property. Once the property is in our possession, it is our choice as to how we will ultimately profit. Very often, we use the lease-option strategy.

However, we could conceivably renovate the property for resale or do a conventional rental. There is nothing inherently special in our lease-optioning our "subject to" mortgage property except that it is our preferred method of profiting.

Having said that, the anticipated plan of how to profit should have been determined much earlier during the stages of due diligence and evaluating the deal.

Our File System

We prepare an Acquisitions file that contains the original borrower's paperwork. Typically, we take most of the paperwork they held when they owned the house. We like to have in our files the past history of the property, including pest service, prior insurance, settlement statement, survey, appraisal, loan paperwork, copy of the deed, and so forth.

We file all the closing paperwork in our Acquisitions file. We typically set up separate files for our Tenants and an ongoing Administrative file for ongoing insurance and monthly statement issues.

Replacing Insurance

If our exit plan is to resell the property quickly, we will not change the insurance. In most cases, we will change the insurance to protect our financial interest in the property. Because we generally keep our properties for cash flow purposes, we most often convert the homeowner policy on the property to a landlord policy. We generally prefer to have a $1,000 deductible.

Many insurance companies will not allow a landlord policy until new tenants have moved in. Sometimes we do not immediately change the insurance policy because of this very reason.

> *"We most often convert the homeowner policy on the property to a landlord policy."*

When we change the insurance, we make sure the lender is listed as the first mortgagee on the policy. We also list the original borrower of the loan on the policy as an interested party. After all, it is his name on that loan.

We also place either our trustee or beneficiary on the policy, depending on the circumstances of the property. It is with this statement I suggest you check with your insurance agent for a recommendation as to who should be listed as the primary insured.

I have heard a variety of answers as to who should be the primary insured. It could be the trustee, the land trust itself, the beneficiary, or the corporate entity that manages or owns the property. The insurance discussion and the intricacies are beyond the scope of my expertise and best left in the hands of insurance professionals.

Summary

The obvious goal of any investment acquisition is completing the closing. However, once a closing ends, there is a new beginning. A series of activities and administrative duties must occur after the closing to ensure the seller's, lender's, and our interests are protected. Once those steps are taken, we quickly move to have the investment property become profitable.

CHAPTER

10

Ongoing Issues

There are important ongoing issues we keep in mind when dealing with any "subject to" mortgage transaction.

At the risk of being repetitive, I cannot emphasize enough that because we are using the seller's loan for the financing, we take special care in managing the account.

Generally, we are proactive in anticipating and solving any problems that may come up regarding the property and the loan itself. For the most part, all that is required to maintain that loan is to make sure timely payments are made and insurance on the property never lapses.

Communication with the Seller

Often, no news is good news where the seller is concerned. If they do not call, it generally means they are not too worried about the loan, especially if we have kept our promise to continue making payments whether we have vacancies or not.

However, over the years, sellers do call in from time to time to see how things are going on our end. When I take the seller's call, I am generally upbeat about hearing from them, and I reassure them that everything is going well. I generally take that opportunity to ask how they are doing since they have moved on. I also ask for their latest forwarding information in case I ever need to contact them.

Sometimes, they want copies of the original paperwork they have either misplaced or did not receive. In those situations, we are happy to comply.

Our communication with the seller is generally minimal unless there is something particular about the property or some piece of historical information we need that is not contained in the paperwork. In those cases, we will call them.

Times Change, Situations Change

As the years go by, we are mindful that as we have grown as a company, the way we did things in the earlier years is somewhat different from the way we do them now. We continue to refine and improve our operations.

Likewise, we are mindful that our sellers' situation may change. But as long as the sellers use and care about their credit, the sellers will always remember us. There is always the chance that having the loan on their credit report can impede any future credit purchase.

> *"As long as the sellers use and care about their credit, the sellers will always remember us."*

On the few occasions that has occurred, we graciously offer to provide a signed letter explaining that while the loan is on the seller's credit report, we bear the financial responsibility for making the payments. We have found a signed letter with a good explanation from us goes a long way to helping the seller overcome credit obstacles. Additionally, it gives us the opportunity to positively reinforce their decision that they did the right thing and dealing with us.

One of the things we don't want to happen is for a seller to suddenly and unexpectedly want the loan to be immediately paid off. We also do not want the seller to complicate our dealings with the lender by interfering or changing things we have set in place.

Property Manager Role

In all our ongoing dealings with lenders, attorneys, insurance agents, and other professionals, we frequently refer to ourselves as "property managers" instead of investors.

The reason we like to refer to ourselves as property managers in dealing with the public is that it implies that we have been given authority by another individual to manage their property and affairs without having to get into the ownership issue. That is backed up by the fact that we have a Power of Attorney signed by the seller giving us the authority to conduct all business relating to a particular property.

> *"We frequently refer to ourselves as 'property managers' instead of investors."*

Lenders are very accustomed to dealing with third-party real estate professionals, such as mortgage brokers, real estate agents, and attorneys, working on the behalf of individual property owners. The property manager title is no different. Referring to ourselves as property managers accurately describes what we do and well positions us to deal with lenders, insurance agents, and other professionals without discussing ownership.

Referring to ourselves as property managers also allows us to take the role of a third-party professional who is interested in doing the right thing for their client. In our case, our "client" is the seller.

> *"It is important to realize that while we may have title to the property, we are simultaneously serving the best interest of our 'clients'."*

It is important to realize that while we may have title to the property, we are simultaneously serving the best interest of our "clients" (sellers) by ensuring that we always have accurate information to make timely payments and adequate property insurance to cover catastrophic loss of the property.

Address Changes & Lost Mail

Despite our best efforts to make sure all correspondence comes to **our** preferred mailing address, occasionally, lender-based mail gets re-routed to the seller's new mailing address. This, of course, is both problematic and very inconvenient because we need to receive all notices, correspondence, and payment books so that we can properly manage the loan.

Address changes are automatically triggered back to the lender if the lender attempts to send correspondence to the borrower and it is then forwarded to the new address. The lender assumes that the forwarding address is the correct address which should be on record.

We can have a lender's mail come to us because of the address change we made once we took over the loan – only to have no more mail come to us when the lender later receives a forwarding address notice.

We have no easy solution to remedy this problem, except to continue monitoring the situation and informing the sellers that they should forward to us any and all mail they might receive from the lender.

Account Changes

Over time, we have dealt with many lenders, and experienced many changes with an account. Sometimes there are minor format changes that occur with newer monthly statements or a new coupon. We become accustomed to what statements look like from each lender and when a change occurs, it is mildly distracting.

More confusing is when the loan servicing company changes. The loan is assigned to another company and the account number changes, the payment address changes, statements change, and the entire customer service channel changes. We watch for this carefully, especially during the transitional stages.

Escrow Account

We find in our "subject to" mortgage deals that there can be wild fluctuations in the escrow account. When we first take over the loan, the escrow account is generally calculated based on a homeowner exemption status.

As such, there is generally a homestead exemption, resulting in lower property taxes. There is also homeowner insurance which is frequently at a lower rate than that of a landlord policy. However, we can sometimes offset this change in rates by asking for a higher deductible in our landlord policy.

> *"When we first take over the loan, the escrow account is generally calculated based on a homeowner status."*

Once a homestead exemption status comes off the property, it is treated as an investment property, and property taxes are escalated. Ultimately, this change raises our monthly payments within a one-year period.

Changes to property taxes and insurance affect the escrow account calculations. When the lender overestimates the amount of funds required, our cash flow suffers. The good news is that we receive the credit later. However, if the lender underestimates the amount of escrow funds required, we can expect an increase in our monthly payments.

Needless to say, we prefer the lender to be as accurate as possible in these calculations. However, we do not have direct control over how the lender determines the escrow account reserve. The best we can do is to monitor the property tax and insurance expenses.

Property Insurance

Of all the issues that annoy me the most, the matter of property insurance tops the list. The insurance industry continues to change, impacting our service expectations. Because "subject to" mortgage transactions are uncommon, insurance agents have a difficult time understanding how to write the policy.

As such, we tend to be proactive with administration of property insurance by making sure that our interests are covered as well as those of the borrowers and the lenders. How we do this is by making sure their names are also on the policy to protect their specific interest in the property.

International Readers

This particular section is specifically directed to readers and investors outside the U.S. I have several friends and acquaintances that are active real estate investors in the countries of Australia, New Zealand, and South Africa. I have also corresponded with investors in Canada and the U.K. In my discussions with them, I have found there are many similarities as well as some differences in the way real estate transactions are conducted. The terminology is sometimes different but many of the concepts are quite similar.

If you have read this entire book, you should realize that even in the U.S., the "subject to" mortgage transaction is not widely understood or supported. It is nevertheless legal and acceptable.

Having said that, I have had discussions with some of my international counterparts and for some the initial reaction to a "subject to" mortgage transaction is, "We can't do that in our country."

My reply to that is "Perhaps. But I do not accept that statement. After all, most Americans also say the same thing here! That it can't be done yet we make it happen. And who says you have to do it the exact way we do it?"

"I am quite certain someone will read this and look for all the reasons why it can't be done."

We make it happen through education, research, perseverance, and only seeking out those who are interested in constructing a legal solution to make things happen.

I am quite certain someone will read this and look for all the reasons why it can't be done. And it will be logical and well-researched. Fine and good for you. It has very little impact on me. I am attempting to help those who are open to interesting possibilities. You find what you seek and you need not read any further. If you want to find a dead end, it won't be hard to do so.

For those of you who are willing to keep an open mind and entertain the idea that perhaps it is possible to implement a similar concept in your country, I will give you some direction to where I would look if I were in your country.

First off, you have to accept the high likelihood you may not be able to do it **exactly** as I have described it. Even within the U.S., the specific implementation and procedure can vary from area-to-area and state-to-state.

The reasons why "subject to" mortgage transactions exist and work has little to do with any one individual, entity, agency, or company "sanctioning" or "giving permission" to do it. It also goes beyond the mechanics. The mechanics were developed piece-by-piece after research was done.

> *"You have to accept the likelihood you may not be able to do it exactly as I describe it."*

I am quite confident that you will not find any legal or contractual clause that specifically gives you permission to do a "subject to" mortgage-like transaction. So, don't waste your time looking.

In that same vein, I am also quite confident that you will not find any legal or contractual verbiage that specifically says and condones the fact you are allowed to eat dinner in the house you bought. No contract or legal instrument will state everything that you can do. But it may say what you can't do.

Unless something is absolutely and specifically forbidden, you can probably find a way or a workaround solution.

If I were in your country, I would focus on finding answers to the following questions. I believe you will get many clues to how you might implement a similar concept in your country.

- What exactly is involved to convey title? Is it a recorded deed? If so, how do deeds get recorded? What are the absolute minimal conditions to have a deed recorded? Details matter. Each step matters.

- What exactly is involved to gain legal possession of a property? You certainly don't need to be an owner to do that. Renters do it all the time.

- How difficult is it to send money to a lender? Can you mail payment in? Or do you have to physically deliver it? Most modern countries allow for checks or electronic form of payment. Do the banks or lenders truly care who submits payments? I am willing to bet that they will take payment from anyone.

- Do banks and lenders like to enforce the law to the point of their detriment? More specifically, will they encourage people to lose property to a foreclosure? Or would they prefer to have someone come up with a creative solution and pay the money?

- Are there some sellers who are unable to sell their property conventionally? If someone were to step in and help them, do you think they might cooperate? Or would they prefer to wait and suffer indefinitely in their circumstance?

- Does seller-financing exist in your country? If so, what are the most common ways seller-financing is implemented? That will give you clues to finding a way to execute creative financing.

I will admit that American culture and American capitalism has a good part in making "subject to" mortgage transactions work. It creates a more willing and open environment to take risks and accept alternative ideas.

However, if you are an International Reader and hope to derive any benefits from this book, the first thing you will have to do is "import" the "can do" attitude. Without that, you will not even be able to begin the research necessary to create a customized "subject to" mortgage or creative financing transaction.

Summary

As the years go by, circumstances will change that will affect our business, our sellers, and the lender. We have ongoing administrative, financial, and managerial responsibilities to ensure that an investment property remains both viable and profitable. We also have to continue ensuring that everyone's interests are protected.

CHAPTER

11

The TurnKey Investing Philosophy

This book was written to provide inside information on how we utilize and implement the "subject to" mortgage strategy to purchase investment properties for our portfolio in our base area of Columbus, Georgia / Phenix City, Alabama. The entire "how to" information we have provided herein is driven by the management philosophy we have adopted and follow. In fact, we refer to it as "The TurnKey Investing Philosophy".

Our philosophy was first shared and written about in *TurnKey Investing with Lease-Options.* We feel it is very important that our readers understand the underlying philosophy which guides our investment actions and decisions. We do not want the information in this manual to be taken out of context or out of the proper perspective. It is simply one tool we use in our overall "TurnKey Investing Philosophy."

Our Strategy

With the exception of my first half-dozen properties, the growth of our portfolio has been accomplished as a joint effort between me and my business partner, Wes Weaver. We accomplish much more as a team than we do separately. We do deals together and manage properties together. We believe in utilizing the concept of "divide-and-conquer" if and when it is appropriate and it serves us well. However, we also firmly adhere to the concept of "strength in numbers" especially when certain situations arise and must be handled.

We've only made small efforts to give insight into how to adapt what we have done in another real estate marketplace. Why? There is simply too much diversity in different real estate markets throughout the United States for any one book or author to cover adequately.

> *"We consider ourselves experts at what we do where we are and nowhere else."*

Therefore, I chose to write about our expertise – the bread-and-butter we actively pursue each and every day and how we do it. Nothing more, nothing less. We consider ourselves experts at what we do where we are and nowhere else. Despite this, I believe astute readers will pick up points and information from this book to apply to their own situations and locations.

Staying Focused

It has been our choice to succeed in our vision with laser-beam focus in the Columbus, Georgia / Phenix City, Alabama area because we wanted to become *"#1 Provider of Owner-Financed Homes"* using lease-options. Using the "subject to" mortgage strategy is one tool we use to acquire investment properties to that end.

Does this mean that if Wes and I were suddenly transplanted to another city, we couldn't learn, master, and become experts there? Of course not. In fact, we feel we could adapt to just about any real estate market if we had to. We believe our experience and achievements can be applied to many real estate markets.

Our TurnKey Investing Philosophy

The reason I bring all this up is to illustrate the major points of what we believe TurnKey Investing is all about.

- Do What You are Good at Doing
- Know Your Market Well
- Invest as a Team, Never Invest Alone
- Management Drives the Success of Every Investment
- Match the Investor to the Investment
- Use a System that Works
- Perfect the System with Kaizen
- Make it Easy for Investors to Invest
- Invest in the Management as much as in the Property.
- Better to Make No Investment Than a Bad Investment
- Always Tell the Bad With the Good
- Be Firm but Fair

Do What You are Good at Doing

One of the dangers we've seen is straying too far away from what you're good at doing. It doesn't mean we cannot be good at more than one thing. Instead, it means we have developed an awareness of the things we can do with great confidence and certainty of success, compared to those things we do with less certainty and greater risk.

There are people in this world who are very good at making money in their businesses but not very good at managing or investing the money they make. These people should recognize this fact and seek out people who are good at managing and investing their money for them.

What we are good at doing is managing and assuring cash flow for investment properties with lease-options in Columbus, Georgia and Phenix City, Alabama. At the risk of sounding boastful, we would be selling ourselves short if we did not acknowledge our success.

Know Your Market Well

We pride ourselves on the fact that we know our real estate market well. We live in a smaller city, making it possible for us to learn and master the marketplace, in contrast to investing in a large city where only a section of the market can be learned and mastered.

In the context of real estate investments, we believe some forms of investing (such as lease-options) are more conducive to certain markets than others. For example, we believe implementing lease-options as an investment strategy favors small to mid-size U.S. cities but not large or highly appreciating cities. **Sometimes it is better to invest money outside of where you live, not where you are.** In my case, I chose to move to a place that was suitable for my investment strategy.

Invest With a Team, Never Invest Alone

Every investment inherently has some level of risk associated with it. There is no such thing as a risk-free investment, just as there is no such thing as risk-free driving. If you get on the road to drive, there is always a small chance you will get into an accident. If you invest, there is always a small chance something will go wrong no matter how many precautions you take.

However, it is important to note risks can be mitigated when more than one person bears the responsibility for an investment. Wes and I have chosen to invest our money together; we have also chosen to manage our properties together. This way, there is always a fallback position.

As I have previously mentioned, it is key to your success to have a team of professionals such as a real estate attorney, local contacts, a banker, a real estate agent, and others in supporting roles.

Management Drives the Success of Every Investment

One of the reasons this book has intentionally been directed to more affluent and sophisticated investors is that they intuitively know that good managers, not the capital itself, drives the success of any business and investment. Poor-minded investors tend to think having money automatically determines the success of investing. If this were true, we would not hear so many stories of rock stars, sports stars, and lottery winners going broke even after coming into millions of dollars.

Having worked in NASCAR circles over ten years ago, I learned that no matter how well a race car is built, how good the engine is, or how fast the car can go, the race is only won with the right driver. It doesn't mean the car is unimportant, but without a great driver, no races are ever won.

Likewise in investing, having access to capital is essential, but without good managers watching and driving the capital and investments, both are doomed to fail.

Match the Investor to the Investment

Because we focus on our expertise within our market, we are cognizant of what we can and cannot do with a potential investor. We also know different people have different priorities and personal dispositions.

While we want to be exposed to many good candidates that may be interested in investing with us, we also know only a select few people will actually be suitable. We have a very specific niche we fill, and only certain investors are suitable for this type of investment.

For example, we now seek "cash-only" investment partners. We rarely seek investors who want to qualify for mortgage loans. Although we will occasionally work with some individuals who prefer to qualify for a loan, it is not our primary focus.

Just as we choose suitable clothes to fit our style, we look for investors who are suitable for our investments. We match the investor to the investments we have.

Use a System That Works

We allocate time to look for ways to improve and streamline our existing system, as well as continue to refine our implementation procedures. At the same time, we are selling lease-options to our tenants. Having said that, once we have developed a good working system for our market, we use it over and over again.

The best example is the way we market our properties through *ownerfinancehomes.com* where we advertise the property, our website, our firm, and our niche simultaneously. It is a very good, cost-effective marketing system that gets better with maturity.

It has worked well, continues to work well, and we continue to expand on it.

Perfect the System with Kaizen

We are firm believers in practicing the Japanese concept of Kaizen. The concept of Kaizen is the belief in making small, ongoing improvements to a business system, which over time, nets great results.

Practicing Kaizen is not always about being the fastest sprinter or making large changes to a system. It is about finishing the marathon as a winner. Sometimes finishing the marathon successfully is not about speed. It is about steadily making progress throughout the entire race.

We are constantly refining how we manage our investment properties, our tenants, and the support team with whom we work.

Make it Easy for Investors to Invest

This is something we are passionate about. We believe investors want to invest their money simply and safely and receive good steady returns on their money. We also believe the investing experience must be a positive one.

Unfortunately, the general nature of real estate makes it somewhat more involved than stock investments. However, this does not mean it has to be a painful experience.

We have two programs we provide to those who want to invest funds with us. One is an "all-cash" Private Lender Program; the other is a "cash plus credit program" Loan Qualification Program, which we only do on a case-by-case basis.

By far, we prefer to work with people on the "all-cash" Private Lender program since it bypasses the tedious mortgage loan qualifying process. While we do everything we can to make the loan qualifying process painless, there are many aspects of the process we cannot control.

With the Private Lender program, we are able to control most of the process, so investing with us is a more positive and pleasant experience.

Invest in the Management as Much as in the Property

There are two ways of looking at this. We have always known that how well we perform as property managers determines how well our investments perform. After all, management drives the success of the investment.

As such, we have committed financial resources to set up more effective management systems. These include management and accounting software. In addition, we also work with vendors who provide services to support our ability to manage. We actively cultivate relationships through familiarity with staff members in the court system and the banks we deal with.

As an investor, you will have many investment opportunities presented to you. However, you should ask yourself the following questions:

- How much access will I have to the principals of the management team?
- Do the principals value their reputation?
- Are they selective with whom they work, or will they work with anyone who has money?
- Do they value working relationships, or do they only value my money?
- Will they go beyond the call of duty?
- How much do the principals have invested with the company and in their portfolio of properties?
- Do they have references and other credibility materials?

- Do they have a strong support network?

Getting answers to these questions will help you make a good decision as to whom you should work with and not solely base the decision on a rate of return. After all, there will be many investment opportunities you will be exposed to which will have similar rates of return. The deciding factor will be the Management Team with whom you choose to work and spend your time.

Better to Make No Investment than a Bad Investment

In the aftermath of the Technology Stocks Crash of 2000, there are many who have been humbled. In 1999, if you offered to pay someone a 5% return on their investment, they probably would have laughed you out the door. Today, if you ask someone who lost money in the years after 2000 if they could go back and earn 5% instead of speculating on stocks, they would jump at the chance. In fact, those who lost tremendously would be more than happy to have broken even with a 0% return. Hindsight is almost always 20/20.

However, this is truly a sad sight to see. The whole point of investing is to create returns, not to hope to break even. Yet that is what many people today are saying. They wish they had broken even so they didn't have to take the loss.

The reality is that they dealt with investment managers who had no control over the market or the investments they were promoting. If those investors had not been overly speculative, they probably would not have lost their money. The fact is that speculative stocks are often bad investments. You either win big or lose big. It sounds like gambling to me.

Fortunately, because of the niche we are in, we do have influence over the marketplace. Even so, we do not offer huge speculative rates of returns. We offer good investments with steady rates of return. It gives us something clear and predictable with which to work. More importantly, the investors get a steady return they can count on, month in and month out. Personally, I think every investment portfolio should have such elements of safety and stability.

Always Tell the Bad with the Good

I have always disliked people who sell a fairy tale story where everything always turns out "happily ever after." They never tell the downside of a story.

In investing, there is always a risk, the downside. The extreme downside is obvious. You could lose all your money! Experienced investors know that investing involves some degree of risk. However, the question is, "What is being done to mitigate the risk?"

Telling the bad side is not about being pessimistic or cynical. Telling the bad side in the context of investing is being upfront with all parties as to the potential risks and downsides of a particular investment. It makes good business sense.

We're upfront and tell both sides of the story. But it still goes without saying that we are clearly confident and optimistic in what we do. (Otherwise, why would we continue to stay in this business?)

Be Firm but Fair

As investment managers and investors ourselves, we have a clear bias towards the investor. Investment partners help fuel the growth of our acquisitions. However, it is our tenants who make an investment perform. So we take them into consideration.

As property managers, we walk a fine line between taking care of the investor and being fair to our tenants. After all, there are rules and laws to abide by with our tenants. Even if this were not the case, our tenants are the people who make the payments which allow our investments to perform.

We are not absolutely ruthless, nor are we unforgiving towards our tenants. Why? Many times it is simply not in our best interest to do so.

We exercise a firm but fair management philosophy not only with our tenants but also with our vendors.

The 6 "S"s of TurnKey Investing

TurnKey Investing is about the 6 basic values that guide what we do. Each of these fundamental values exists within our preferred method of real estate investing: the Lease-Options Strategy.

Simple
For investing to be a turnkey system, it has to be *simple to understand* and *simple to implement*. Most importantly, it has to be *simple to invest* in.

Safety
Turnkey investing is about *safety*, not speculation or "sexiness" of the idea. Turnkey investing creates *safety* through experience, certainty, and risk management.

Steady
Turnkey investing is about delivering *steady performance*. It is about carrying out essential activities in an even-keeled, consistently, steady way. It is about avoiding dazzle and drama in the day-to-day activities.

Security
The way we protect our investment partners in turnkey investing is about offering *security (collateral)*, not just a promise or a good story. With real estate, the investment property is often the back-end security to a *secure* investment plan.

Spendable
Within our investment portfolio, our turnkey investments generate *spendable cash flow* each and every month. This is not perceived equity or compounding the returns. We create *spendable returns* for ourselves and our investment partners. They can *choose* how to deploy the spendable returns they receive.

Systems
Turnkey investing is about creating and developing a *duplicatable system* of tasks that can be used over and over. We create and execute a *management, marketing, and investing system* with a turnkey philosophy in mind.

Summary

Within every successful investment portfolio, there is a winning philosophy that guides the actions of the management team. We are no different. As the title of the book indicates, we advocate a “turnkey” approach to doing things. More specifically, we have developed a turnkey system of doing lease-options; it works for our investment partners and for us.

Our portfolio continues to perform well, month in and month out. And while there are occasional setbacks both in management and performance, we are happy to report success in our ventures.

Our *TurnKey Investing Philosophy* allows for both change and growth, and it helps keep us grounded. We believe every successful management team should put into writing a management philosophy that they can share with others. It helps the management team to be accountable to themselves and the people with whom they work. In the end, it is all about setting the right expectations for all involved and then delivering solid results.

Conclusion

For many people, acquiring investment property is the end objective. But for Wes and me, the acquisition of any investment property is only the beginning of a long-term project that can span years and even decades. The business of building an investment portfolio and having it perform year after year is a long-term project.

Many properties we acquired were in fact purchased and financed with "subject to" mortgages. It has been a successful and highly educational endeavor. As of this writing, every property we bought with a "subject to" mortgage continues to perform profitably. Of course, some perform better than others. That will always be the case when you are continually acquiring properties as we are.

"Subject to" mortgages are like medication. "Subject to" mortgages are great for solving certain challenges. But it is not a magical cure-all for investment challenges. We use it with care and we use it responsibly. And there are side effects to be aware of.

Ultimately, we wonder how these properties bought with "subject-to" mortgages will turn out 10, 15, and 20 years out. Will these "subject-to" mortgages go the distance? Or will we eventually have to liquidate or refinance these properties? Quite honestly, we don't know, but we keep a watchful eye. We remain vigilant and stay prepared to make changes.

The challenge of writing any real estate investment book is trying to take a complicated and tedious subject, with many moving and ever-changing elements, and distilling it into a comprehensible 200-page book.

I have attempted to paint a realistic picture. I was going to also say a 'complete picture,' but then I realized there is no such thing. This book is only a snapshot of where we have been and how we currently do things. Nothing more.

I hope you have been able to pick and choose the information that best suits your situation and local market. What we do is simply that. It is what we do. The idea is not to exactly emulate what we do. The idea should be to adapt the information we have presented to your own needs.

Nevertheless, I trust this book has been helpful to you. If you have thoughts and constructive comments you would like to share with me, or if I can answer some of your questions, I invite you to contact me.

Thank you for reading this book. Until we meet again, may all your investments be simple, safe, and steady.

Matthew S. Chan

APPENDIX A

Sample Documents

LIMITED POWER OF ATTORNEY

BE IT KNOWN, that I do hereby grant a limited and specific power of attorney to: **OUR TRUSTEE's NAME**.

He shall have full power and authority to handle any and all lawful transactions involving Real Estate Property known as: **123 ABC Street, Anywhere, USA 12345.**

The authority herein shall include, but not limited to, the full power to contract to sell or lease at any terms, convey the real estate with or without consideration, manage and maintain the property, make repairs or renovations, inquire and modify insurance and loan information, issue payments, and any other incidental acts that are reasonably required to carry out and perform these duties.

My Trustee agrees to accept this appointment subject to its terms, and agrees to act and perform on my behalf in his discretion as deems advisable. This power of attorney is effective upon execution until the final closing of the property.

Signed under seal this ____ day of __________, 2005.

____

Property Seller Signature

Disclaimer: *This sample document has been provided for educational purposes. We assume no liability whatsoever for any direct or indirect consequences for use of this sample document.*

Cancellation Notice to Insurance Company

Date: __________, 2005

Insurance Co: ________________________
Policy #: ____________________________
Property Address: **123 ABC Street, Anywhere, USA**

Dear Customer Service:

Effective immediately, please cancel the property insurance on the aforementioned property. I have made arrangements to have this policy replaced with another policy with a different company and agent.

Please redirect any remaining correspondence and insurance refunds to:

456 Our Office Street, Anywhere, USA

Please note that my property managers, Joe Blow, may call to followup on this matter. You can reach them at 123-456-7890.

Thank you for your cooperation in this matter.

Sincerely,

____
Property Seller Signature

Disclaimer: *This sample document has been provided for educational purposes. We assume no liability whatsoever for any direct or indirect consequences for use of this sample document.*

Seller Information Sheet

Seller Name: ______________________________
Address: ______________________________
City/State/ZIP: ______________________________

Phone
Home #: ______________
Work #: ______________
Mobile #: ______________

#BR / #BA: ______________
How long Occupied: ______________

Square Footage: ______________
Age of Property: ______________

Property Status: Owner-occupied / Rental / Vacant

Condition of Property: Excellent / Good / Fair / Poor

Repairs & Maintenance Needed: ______________________________________

Seller's FMV: $______________
Our FMV: $______________

1st Lender: ______________________________________
Monthly Pymt: $______________ Balance: $ ______________
Arrearage: $______________ Interest: __________%

2nd Lender: ______________________________________
Monthly Pymt: $______________ Balance: $ ______________
Arrearage: $______________ Interest: __________%

Reason for Selling: ______________________________
Cash seller Needs: $______________
Planned Move Date: ______________

Disclaimer: *This sample document has been provided for educational purposes. We assume no liability whatsoever for any direct or indirect consequences for use of this sample document.*

APPENDIX

B

Area Maps

Regional Map

(Columbus, Georgia & Phenix City, Alabama Area)

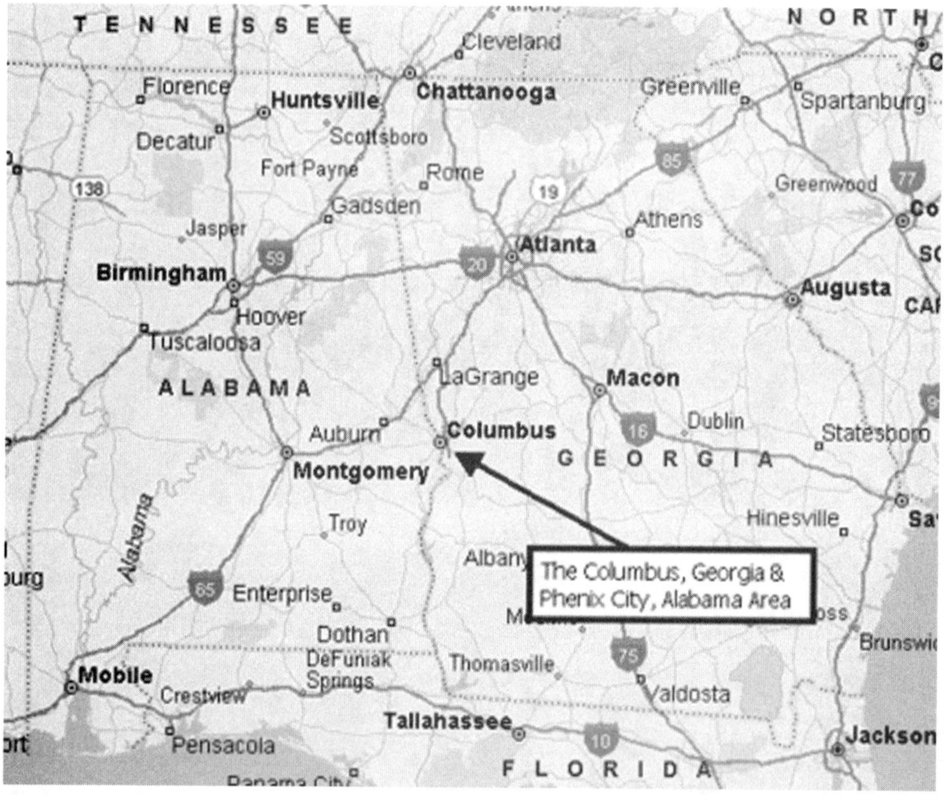

The Greater Columbus Area

(Columbus, Georgia & Phenix City, Alabama)

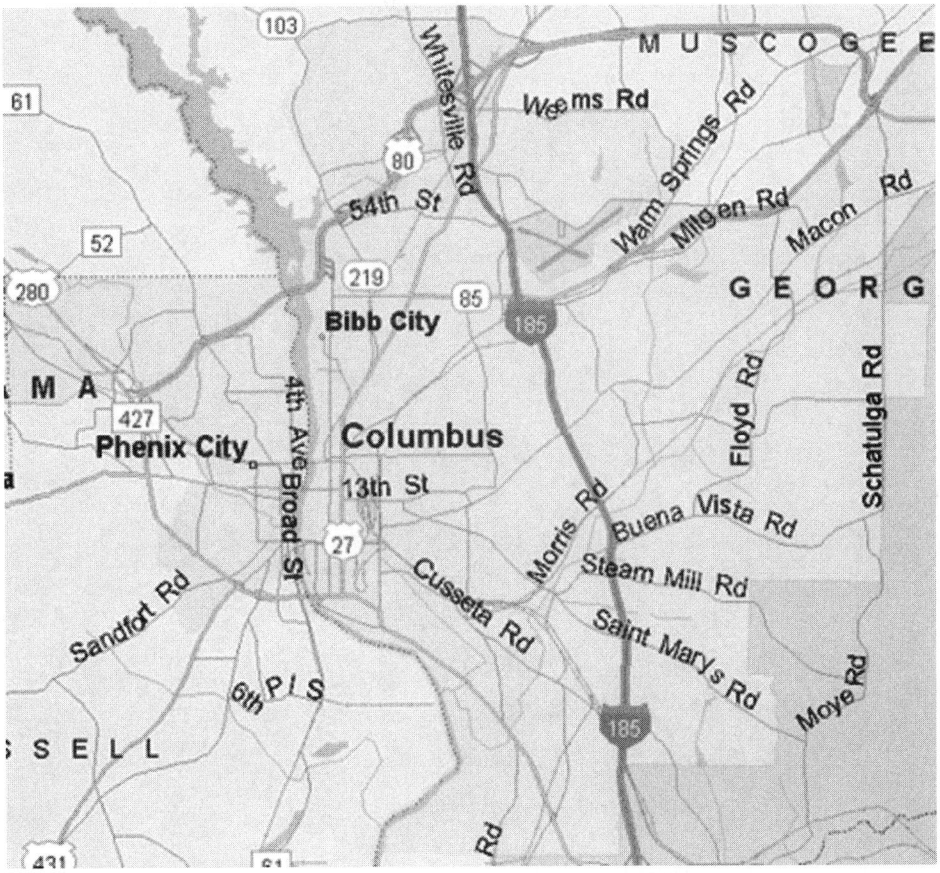

APPENDIX C

Property Photos

Sample Alabama Houses Purchased with "Subject to" Mortgage

Sandfort Rd, (3-BR / 2-BA) FMV: $80,000

Bleeker Rd, (3-BR / 1-BA) FMV: $45,000

Red Oak Dr, (3-BR / 1.5-BA) FMV: $55,000

Lee Road 240, (3-BR / 2-BA) FMV: $110,000

Lee Road 2041, (3-BR / 2-BA) FMV: $85,000

Sample Georgia Houses Purchased with "Subject to" Mortgage

Blueridge Dr, (3-BR / 1-BA) FMV: $60,000

Lawyers Lane, (3-BR / 1-BA) FMV: $45,000

Vesper Dr, (3-BR / 1-BA) FMV: $75,000

Goodwin Dr, (3-BR / 2-BA) FMV: $110,000

Celia Dr, (3-BR / 1-BA) FMV: $75,000

Acknowledgements

I most want to recognize my friend, business partner, and lead contributor of this book, Wes Weaver. Wes is the man who is most responsible for helping me create and implement the "turnkey" into "TurnKey Investing". Without his help, I could not have accomplished what I have done today. Nor could I have written this book.

With Wes at my side, I am proud to say we have made a formidable team in the Greater Columbus, Georgia area. This book is a testament to his huge contributions to our business and investments. I thank Wes for coming into my life those years ago to support me both personally and professionally today.

There are other people I would like to acknowledge:

To the teachers who have most influenced and impacted me on this "subject to" mortgage handbook project with their business acumen, technical knowledge, and investment wisdom. Their combined teachings helped shape the "subject to" mortgage acquisition style I use today. I thank Bill Bronchick and Ron Legrand.

To my investor friends who continue to support my investment ventures with their advice and encouragement. Their friendship continues to inspire and propel me forward by leaps and bounds in ways they do not even realize. I thank Joe Arlt, Troy Arment, Craig Chandler, Steve Copper, Dean Edelson, Fred & Marleen Geyen, Bill Gordon, Greg & Felicity Heffernan, Jerry & Lisa Hoganson, Damion Lupo, Brad & Cindy Simmons, and Chad Watson.

To our real estate attorney, Karen Earley, for her ongoing legal support of our business. We could not do what we do so well without her insights and commitment to always getting the job done.

To those special friends who support me and my business in their own unique way. I thank John Burley, Cindy Chapin, Melita Hunt, P.J. Zwart, and Robert Yang.

To the friends who are continually interested in what I do in my business life no matter what I do. They provide ongoing optimism for any work I do. I thank Ryan Stewart, Beverly Weaver, Paolo Bruno, Jack Williams, and Perry & Darla Anderson.

Creative Team

The author often receives the sole recognition and credit for the finished book. People think the author did all the work. Nothing can be further from the truth. I would like to recognize those individuals who helped me make this book possible.

First, I want to recognize my cover designer, Cheryl Edwards, for continuing to create cover art that is both stunning and eye-catching. Her sense of creativity and insights remain consistent to my sense of tradition. Cheryl, I thank you and I appreciate you for your ongoing support of my book projects.

Second, I want to recognize my typesetter and desktop publisher, Deanna Reynolds, for helping me transform the text I wrote into an organized, readable handbook format. Deanna, I thank you for your continued enthusiasm and quick responses in putting this handbook together.

Third, I want to recognize my editor, LaRue Foster, for making sense of my writings and smoothing out the many rough spots in my manuscript. LaRue, I thank you for your organization, enthusiasm, and sense of patience.

Finally, I want to thank my assistant, Richelle Tomlins, for her enthusiasm, feedback, and completing the very necessary and important final manuscript review.

To the members of the creative team, I salute them for helping me produce this book.

I recommend each of these talented individuals. You can contact them at:

Cheryl Edwards
Cover Designer / Graphic Artist
http://www.ouidzine.com

Deanna Reynolds
Typsetter / Desktop Publisher
deannareynolds@verizon.net

LaRue Foster
Editor
lfoster@earthlink.net

About the Author

Matthew Chan is the author of "The TurnKey Investor's 'Subject To' Mortgage Handbook", an alternative financing book that teaches independent-minded investors how to buy investment property without qualifying for a loan using a little-known seller-financing technique.

Matthew has been involved with investment real estate through family rental property since he was a teen-ager! After spending ten years in Corporate America, Matthew escaped to become a successful entrepreneur at the age of 29. A few short years later, he started his own investment real estate portfolio. Today, that highly profitable and expanding portfolio consistently generates spendable cash flow for himself and his investment partners.

Along with launching new book projects and speaking with new investment partners, Matthew continues to oversee the management of his Internet businesses and his real estate management company.

Matthew continues to enjoy the freedom of spending time working only on projects and investments with people he likes. His business and investment interests continue to take him across the U.S. where he frequently meets and networks with new people.

Matthew is also the author of "TurnKey Investing with Lease-Options" and "The Intrepid Way" book series. That book series teaches employees how to leave the confines of the corporate world through entrepreneurship.

Matthew's educational background includes a Bachelor of Science in Business Administration from University of Central Florida, and a Masters of Business Administration from Webster University.

About the Contributor

Wes Weaver is the lead contributor of two books, "The TurnKey Investor's 'Subject To' Mortgage Handbook" and "TurnKey Investing with Lease-Options". These books teach independent-minded investors how to use a turnkey system approach in their investment activities.

With a state-approved work permit in hand at age 15, Wes had an early start in building his character, maturity, and discipline, working for different businesses throughout high school and college. Working his way up, Wes became at 21, one of the youngest commissioned salesperson in the food distribution industry.

Having achieved annual sales of over $1.3 million for his employer, Wes left the corporate world at the age of 24 to become a real estate investor. Through his property management firm, Wes invests in real estate for himself and his investment partners. Today, Wes continues to enjoy the passive income generated by his real estate portfolio.

Wes recently became a Real Estate Agent which helps streamline the acquisition of new investment properties for his team. He is occasionally a guest speaker at special educational events. Seeking ongoing growth and education, Wes often travels and networks with entrepreneurs and investors outside of his area to bring fresh perspectives into his business. Through his contacts in the U.S., he continues to expand his knowledge base which he applies to his business.

About the Management Team

Matthew Chan & Wes Weaver are the principals of Intrepid Capital Group, a privately-held management firm based in Columbus, Georgia.

Shortly after Matthew's move into Columbus, Matthew and Wes began a friendship that eventually led them to forge an alliance to buy, invest, and manage investment property together.

With focus and determination, Matthew and Wes have established themselves as the "#1 Providers of Owner-Financed Homes" in the Greater Columbus, Georgia area. They specialize in selling single-family homes with "owner-financing" with their innovative TurnKey Lease-Options system.

Matthew and Wes have mastered the art and science of generating safe and steady returns through investment properties in their local area. The TurnKey Lease-Options System they implement is a customized Marketing & Management System they use to great strategic advantage.

Matthew and Wes take a deliberate tag-team approach to their management style. They often carry out a "divide and conquer" strategy but also come together when a "strength in numbers" style is required. Their unorthodox but effective management style allows them to create a management synergy that few individuals in their local area can match.

Backed by their support team and advisors, they are steadfast and decisive in their approach of buying, investing, and managing cash flow investment properties.

In these turbulent economic times, Matthew and Wes continue to be pillars of stability for their investment partners. The mantra they practice and implement is, "Safe and steady returns through ongoing cash flow."

Recommended Resources

Books I Recommend to Expand Your Investment Mind:

"All About Escrow and Real Estate Closings"
by Sandy Gadow
Brief: The mechanics of real estate closings in easy-to-read language

"Barron's Real Estate Handbook"
by Jack Harris & Jack Friedman
Brief: Reference manual with real estate terms, definitions, & diagrams

"Every Landlord's Legal Guide"
by M. Stewart, R. Warner, et al.
Brief: A good landlord guide and information resource on all 50 states

"Places Rated Almanac"
by David Savageau
Brief: Excellent overview of over 300 U.S. city profiles & demographics

"Real Estate Quick and Easy"
by Roy Maloney
Brief: Real estate concepts described with simple text and illustrations

"TurnKey Investing with Lease-Options"
by Matthew S. Chan
Brief: The turnkey system we use to lease-option properties out for cash flow

"The Intrepid Way"
by Matthew S. Chan
Brief: Using the entrepreneurial lifestyle to create personal freedom

"The Intrepid Way II - Transformation"
by Matthew S. Chan
Brief: Personal changes you must make to live the entrepreneurial lifestyle

Websites I Recommend:

Chamber of Commerce http://www.chamberofcommerce.com
Brief: Market research tool to locate Chambers of Commerce in the U.S.

Cornell University's Legal Information Institute
http://www.law.cornell.edu/topics/state_statutes3.html#property
Brief: State statutes on property law

HUD's Fair Housing Laws & Presidential Executive Orders
http://www.hud.gov/offices/fheo/FHLaws/index.cfm
Brief: Fair housing laws for property managers and landlords

U.S. Housing Market Analysis by the Meyers Group
http://www.housingusa.com
Brief: Housing market analysis overview of the U.S.

U.S. Census Bureau http://www.census.gov
Brief: Excellent market research tool provided by the U.S. government

PropertyBoss http://www.propertyboss.com
Brief: The property management software we use

QuickBooks http://www.quickbooks.com
Brief: The accounting software we use

TurnKey Investing http://www.turnkeyinvesting.com
Brief: The companion website to this book

OwnerFinanceHomes.com
http://www.ownerfinancehomes.com
Brief: Our primary website for marketing our properties

ProHomeBuyers.com http://www.prohomebuyers.com
Brief: Our primary website for buying "subject to" mortgage properties

Ascend Beyond Publishing http://www.ascendbeyond.com
Brief: The publisher of TurnKey Investing series of books

Bonus Book Excerpt:

TurnKey Investing with Lease-Options

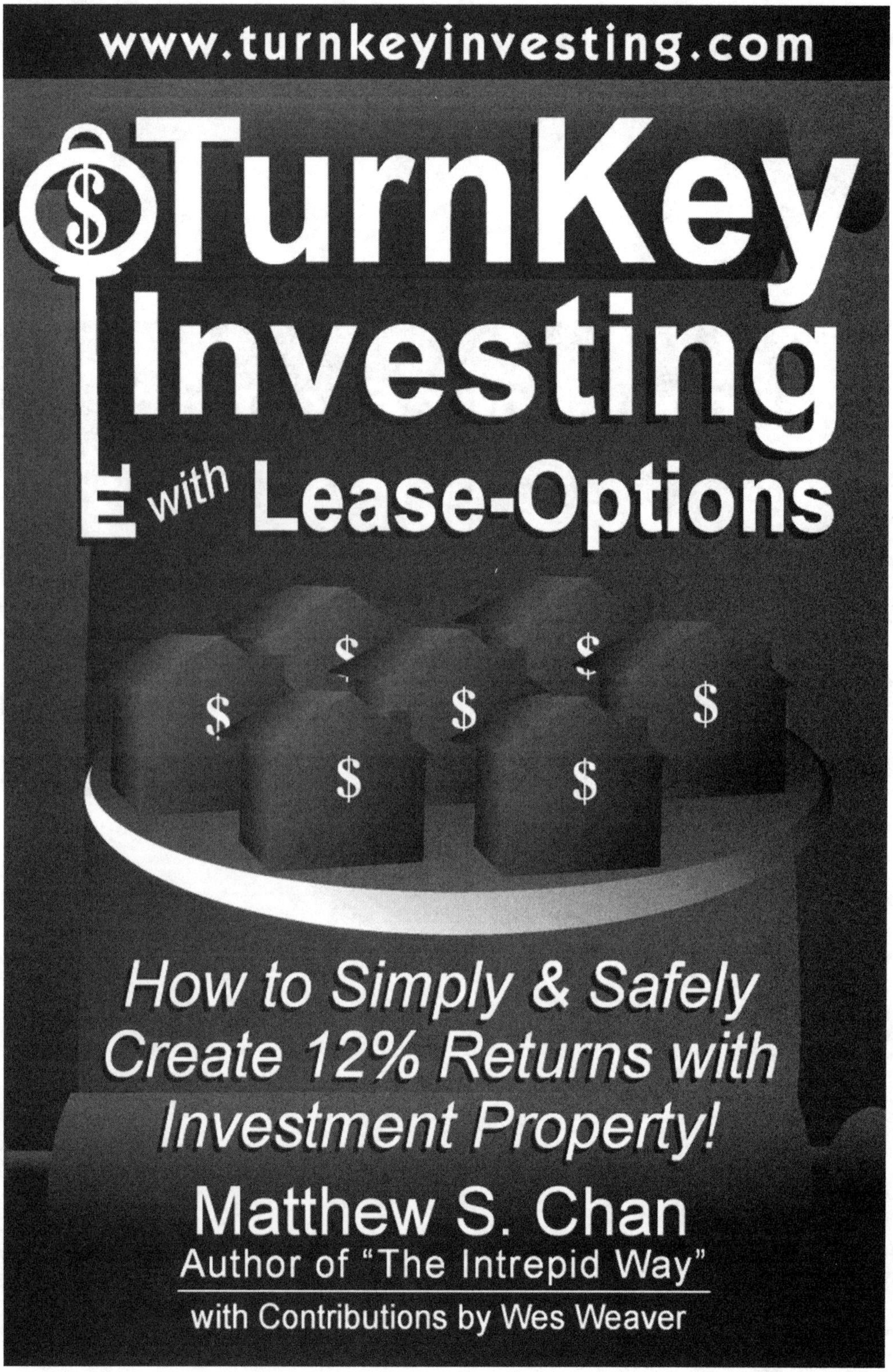
www.turnkeyinvesting.com
TurnKey
Investing
with Lease-Options
How to Simply & Safely
Create 12% Returns with
Investment Property!
Matthew S. Chan
Author of "The Intrepid Way"
with Contributions by Wes Weaver

Introduction

In April 2000, the Technology Stocks Crash of 2000 began a three-year decline that erased trillions of dollars of investor wealth leaving dead companies and crushed retirement accounts in its wake.

As a result, the U.S. economy plummeted with the steepest decline in recent memory. Millions of jobs were lost. Unemployment climbed. Bankruptcies and foreclosures escalated. Investment and retirement accounts were decimated.

Out of all this, I am both happy and relieved to say that I was not one of these unfortunate victims.

In January 2000, I converted all my mutual fund holdings into a cash position. When the crash occurred three months later, I knew I had made the right decision to liquidate.

While some people may simply say I was lucky, there were clear indications that a crash would occur in the near future. The problem was I did not have a crystal ball to tell me exactly when it would happen. Nevertheless I escaped unscathed.

How did I manage to escape?

The Escape

In late 1999, I experienced an unusual decline in my mutual funds portfolio. While it was not the first decline I experienced that year, it was unusual because I began to realize that my allegedly stable mutual fund portfolio was becoming more volatile with each passing month.

And since the volatility of mutual funds went against everything I was taught about how mutual funds worked the previous 15 years, it seemed to me something was wrong. Very wrong. So I decided to do the only thing I knew how to do at the time. Liquidate and escape from the stock market so I could re-evaluate future investment plans.

The Change

With no expertise or experience in the stock market, I turned my investing activities to another direction. I chose to invest in small houses to produce cash flow. While many so-called investors like to buy and fix-up houses for resale, it is not what I consider true investing. That business is called property renovation. It is what many car dealers do. They buy old cars, fix them up, and resell them. They make money but it isn't investing. It is a job. The pay stops with that one transaction.

I was looking for ongoing, spendable cash flow I could count on month in, month out until I grew old. I knew once I built up a portfolio of investment property, I could stop acquiring properties at any time and not sacrifice ongoing income.

In 1999, I bought a couple of small investment houses. Although I had dealt with family rental property and rental contracts as a teenager, I was still relatively inexperienced. It is a very different experience to buy and manage your own investment property.

The Move

After a slow start and a big move to the smaller city of Columbus, Georgia, I began to quickly learn the art and science of creating a profitable system of investing that worked in my new home city. I learned through a combination of research, teachers, investor friends, seminars, courses, books, and, yes, hard-core *field experience.*

With each property I acquired and every tenant I placed, I got better at the real estate investing and management process. After a few months living in Columbus, Georgia and making a few more acquisitions, I met someone who first became my apprentice, then my friend, and eventually my business and management partner. His name is Wes Weaver. I am proud to have him as the Lead Contributor of this book.

The Growth

Since our alliance, Wes and I have gone on to acquire and manage three dozen properties for cash flow using our turnkey lease-option system.

In layman terms, we buy small investment houses and resell them with owner-financing. We collect a small "down payment" and receive monthly payments from our tenants. We have no ongoing maintenance or repair expenses. We do very little fix up of properties, if any. And if these tenants stop paying, we have them removed and then repeat the selling process with minimal expense and effort.

We have developed our own "recipe", our own "cookie-cutter" investment system, which we call TurnKey Investing. More specifically, we do TurnKey Investing with Lease-Options.

The How-To Guide

Quite frankly, the information contained in this book is not a gold-mine, but a platinum-mine of information. To date, there is no book quite like this one with all the details and inside secrets we share. Some of the hard-to-find information we provide in this book came at a cost of years of experience and thousands of dollars. This book is easily worth 100 times the cover price.

Wes and I generate several thousands of dollars of spendable income for ourselves and investment partners. We are proud of this fact. Our investment partners often do not have the time, expertise, or inclination to do it themselves. You will see later in the book, how we make money from buying these small investment houses and lease-optioning them out.

This book was written for a variety of reasons:

First, because of our lead position in our market niche and the number of investment properties we manage for others, more and more people we know have become interested in learning what we do, and more importantly, how we do it.

Second, because we invite investment partners to work with us, this book allows us to more completely and efficiently communicate what we do without all the fluff of a brochure.

Third, as our management team grows, this book serves as both an instructional and operational guide into what and how we do things. It is a more concise alternative to a full-scale Operations Manual.

Finally, for those people who choose to manage their own real estate investment portfolios, this book will be an invaluable guide to implementing the lease-option strategy in their own markets.

Chapter 1 - The Beauty of Lease-Options

The Benefits of Lease-Options

There are many benefits to using lease-options as a strategy to manage a portfolio of investment property. As an investor, our emphasis is to improve portfolio performance by increasing returns, reducing volatility, and lowering the overall risk.

The following characteristics make lease-options more favorable than conventional landlording:

- More Upfront Money
- Higher Rents
- Higher Sales Price
- Little or No Maintenance Costs
- Attracts Better Tenants
- Flexible Use
- Less Management Responsibilities
- Quick Tenant Removal When They Default
- Tax Benefits
- Alternative Financing

Most of these benefits come from the tenant mindset that they are "buying" a property where the lease-option becomes a form of intermediate financing. With this short-term intermediate financing, the goal is to obtain a refinance loan with another lender to ultimately own the property. Because of the buyer's mindset, tenants are willing to pay more and do more for the opportunity to buy.

More Upfront Money

There is almost always greater upfront money received from lease-option tenants than is normally collected with a standard rental. The tenants are willing to provide more upfront money because they view the funds they are paying as similar to a down payment in a conventional purchase with a mortgage. Because their intent is to ultimately own the property, they are willing to give extra upfront money to secure the right to purchase the property.

Higher Rents

Because few property investors are willing to sell and provide financing to the type of people we deal with, they are willing to pay a higher monthly premium for the right to buy. As such, we are able to collect higher rent payments than normally allowed through conventional rentals. It is not uncommon to receive monthly payments that are 10%-20% higher than prevailing market rents.

Higher Sales Price

In addition to the willingness to pay higher rents, the tenants are willing to pay a higher price for the property as well. The price is often secondary as long as they can afford the upfront money and the monthly rent payments.

People in this socio-economic group are simply not as discriminating in the price they pay for a property. Most are simply happy to have someone willing to sell a house to them and provide intermediate financing to do so. This sense of gratitude makes them very receptive to paying a higher price.

Little or No Maintenance Costs

When people buy houses, it is unsaid but understood that once someone buys a house, they have to assume the repair and maintenance responsibilities for that house. Because all parties are clear in the arrangement that the tenants are ultimately buying the property, it is expected they will take responsibility for all repairs and maintenance since it will become their house. To real estate investors, this point is one of the major benefits in using lease-options. Short of catastrophic damage to the property, the investor can expect nearly no maintenance or repair costs compared to those with standard rentals.

Attracts Better Tenants

The people who are attracted to lease-options are often those who have already rented for many years. They have attempted to buy a house through conventional means, but for a variety of reasons, they have been unable to do so.

Because they have rented for many years, our tenants are frustrated homebuyers looking for someone to give them an opportunity to buy with easy financing. Because many have tried to qualify for conventional mortgages, they are aware of the need for a down payment. As such, these people often have a good tenant history, are employed, and have accumulated a decent amount of savings to put towards a down payment. In our case, this is upfront money to be used for a lease-option arrangement.

Flexible Use

Typically, in a conventional rental situation, the landlord is expected to provide housing that includes functional appliances, functional environmental systems, reasonably good flooring/carpeting, landscaping, and a good interior condition. Not only are landlords expected to provide tenants this at the time of move-in, but the landlord is also expected to incur the cost of ongoing maintenance and repairs! All this so that he can collect only a small security deposit and first month's rent!

When the tenants enter into a lease-option transaction, they understand that they are "buying" into the property in "as is" condition. It does not mean that we, as investors, don't do some property preparation. However, it also doesn't mean that it is necessary to totally renovate a property before we can "sell" it. Often, you can "sell" the property "as is" with all its imperfections.

Less Management Responsibilities

Once an investment property has been "sold" through a lease-option transaction, there are almost no management responsibilities except to ensure that the monthly payment is received. The repair and maintenance responsibilities have been placed with the tenant. As such, most of the well known "landlord headaches" have been removed.

Quick Tenant Removal When They Default

The lease-option transaction, when structured correctly, often utilizes prevailing landlord-tenant laws of eviction to resolve cases of non-payment. With alternative forms of financing, the investor often has to resort to a foreclosure process, which can be both time-consuming and expensive.

The goal of eviction is three-fold. The first is to have the tenants removed from the property. The second is to get legal possession of the property. And the third is to get a judgment so additional collection measures, such as garnishment or levy of personal property, may be pursued.

When the tenant stops paying either voluntarily or involuntarily, having a quick repossession is paramount to getting the investment property performing again. The eviction process is the quickest and most cost-effective way to do this. With legal possession, we can take actions to once again get our investment property performing.

Tax Benefits

Monthly income from investment property under a lease-option agreement is generally considered to be rental income. Rental income generally falls under the category of "passive activity income" within the view of the IRS, which is taxed lower than personal service income (earned income).

Further, some of the upfront money collected such as security deposits can be tax-deferred until the day the landlord claims the money for compensation for damages or losses. Additionally, option money can be tax-deferred until the tenant either leaves the property or exercises the option, whichever comes first.

If the property is sold after 12 months of ownership, it is generally taxed at long-term capital gains rates, which are often much lower than earned income rates. Additionally, if advanced notice is provided, investors need not take the profits. The IRS allows property investors to do a tax-deferred "1031 exchange" so that all the profits are rolled into another property of "like-kind".

Note: As in the case of all taxation matters, you should consult a CPA or other expert financial counsel.

Alternative Financing

Many lenders and investors recognize lease-option transactions as a form of owner-financing. It gives the tenant full use of the property, but also the right to buy. This can be a favorable arrangement for both tenant and landlord. When done correctly, both parties' interests are fulfilled.

Since the lease-option transaction is often recognized as a form of owner-financing, it often facilitates greater ease in getting a new loan for the tenant so he can successfully buy the property and ultimately have title transferred into his name.

Misconceptions of Lease-Options

I often encounter investors who are conventional landlords. It seems no matter how much I try to explain the benefits of lease-option transactions to them, they never quite grasp the benefits. As such, writing this book allows me the opportunity to clarify any misconceptions.

The first step for conventional landlords is to have an open mind when it comes to investing. Never have I said, don't consider conventional landlording; it simply means by understanding lease-options, you will have an additional instrument within your investment repertoire.

Misunderstanding and resistance to lease-option transactions center on the following issues:

- The investors need for ownership "forever"
- Misunderstanding the mindset of lease-option tenants
- Ignorance of multiple profit centers

Buy and Hold Forever

People from a conventional landlording background often "buy and hold" property for life. The underlying motivation for them is to one day fully own the property "free and clear." They are primarily working for the future, and may or may not receive a lot of upfront money or monthly cash flow from their tenants. Their mindset says they are willing to sacrifice some of the money because their tenants will "pay their mortgage" until the day they own it "free and clear." They simply don't want any possibility of "losing" the property.

If the owners do hold the investment for monthly cash flow, conventional "buy and hold" investors fear they will lose the monthly income once it is sold. Along with the fear of loss of monthly income is the fear of not being able to find a replacement property.

What "buy and hold" investors fail to understand is that most people who enter into a lease-option agreement never fully exercise their option to buy. This is not by our design. It simply is the nature of the types of tenants that are attracted to owner-financing. They either stop paying or simply move on. If and when the property comes back to us, we can increase the upfront money, the monthly rent, and the option price to better reflect changes in the market.

This is analogous to the homebuyers of today who take on 30-year mortgages. Relatively few such mortgages live out their entire 30-year lifespan. It is commonly known in the lending industry that the average American will move every five to seven years, and when they do, they get a new 30-year loan.

Tenants who agree to lease-option agreements have the *intention* of staying with the property for a long time. However, the very reasons they were unable to buy a house conventionally are often the reasons that compel them to move on. Their track record of personal stability has not been established long enough to allow them to buy conventionally.

We give our tenants the benefit of the doubt that they want to buy, but our experience has shown that most will move on within three years. Like conventional landlording, there is turnover with lease-option transactions. However, the biggest difference between the two, is that we are often financially rewarded when turnover occurs while conventional landlords are not.

Ultimately, we expect most of the houses we have in our portfolio to be paid off by our chain of lease-option tenants over the course of the next 30 years. And on the off-chance a tenant successfully exercises his option to buy, through qualifying for a refinance loan, there is nothing difficult in rolling the realized equity forward into an equivalent replacement property.

Misunderstanding the Tenant Mindset

Generally speaking, investors who are accustomed to old-fashioned "buy and hold" often do not understand the mindset of lease-option tenants.

"Buy and hold" investors do not understand that psychologically, the desire for tenants to own a home is extremely high. It is a fundamental dream of most societies. As such, these people are willing to pay more, do more, and assume responsibility unheard of among conventional tenants.

This is the mindset that "buy and hold" investors fail to understand, but ultimately this is what translates into higher returns, better performance and fewer management challenges within our investment portfolio.

When tenants are willing to pay more and do more on all levels, it inevitably translates to better investment performance.

Tenants realize there are mostly "buy and hold" investors in the market, which makes it more competitive. In the lease-options market, we have virtually no direct competition.

In my view, "buy and hold" investors miss the opportunity to capitalize on the fundamental desire of home ownership within most tenants. In the end, it is unlikely our tenants will have the personal stability to ultimately own the property, and this often works out in our best interest.

Multiple Profit Centers

Closely related to how "buy and hold" investors do not understand the mindset of lease-option tenants, is how they cannot understand there are potentially three profit centers from a lease-option transaction instead of one.

"Buy and hold" investors are mostly focused on the monthly rents. However, in a lease-option agreement, there are potentially three profit centers.

- Upfront money
- Higher monthly payment
- Back-end Option

Typically, in a conventional rental, the upfront money received comes in the form of a security deposit and first month's rent. In the way we do lease-options, our upfront money typically consists of a security deposit, an administrative fee, prorated first month's rent, and option money.

Profit Center 1 - Upfront Money

The greater upfront money we receive from a tenant comes from their willingness to pay the equivalent of a "low down payment". The upfront money typically covers three months worth of vacancy. If we move a property within two months, we actually come out ahead with the tenant turnover.

On top of all of this, we typically do not bring the property to prime condition as we might do with a conventional rental. Later on in the book, I will explain what we do to prepare the property for "resale." I can assure you, however, that they are mostly low-expense items. Our tenants take on the responsibility of repainting, wallpapering, getting appliances, carpeting, flooring, and performing minor repairs.

It is important to note, if we subscribed only to "buy and hold," we would receive relatively little upfront money, AND we would also have to spend far more for selling the property in renovated condition.

Comparison of Lease-Option vs. Conventional Rental

3-bedroom, 1-bath house
Market Rent = $500.00, Monthly P.I.T.I. = $375.00

Lease-Option		Conventional Rental	
House cleaning:	$ 50.00	House cleaning:	$ 50.00
Yard care:	$ 50.00	Yard care:	$ 50.00
Carpet cleaning:	$ None	Carpet cleaning:	$ 100.00
Paint:	$ None	Paint:	$ 100.00
Appliances:	$ None	Appliances:	$ 200.00
Total Preparation Expense:	$ 100.00	Total Preparation Expense:	$ 700.00

Lease-Option preparations cost less!

Lease-Option		Conventional Rental	
Administrative Fee:	$ 200.00	Application Fee:	$ 20.00
Security Deposit:	$ 250.00	Security Deposit:	$ 350.00
Prorated 1st month:	$ 250.00	1st Month's Rent:	$ 500.00
Option Money:	$ 900.00		
Total Upfront Money:	$1,600.00	Total Upfront Money:	$ 870.00

More upfront money with a Lease-Option!

Profit Center 2 – Higher monthly payment

As I mentioned, because lease-option tenants are willing to make monthly payments that are typically higher than market rents AND are willing to take on the maintenance and repairs responsibility, we do not receive calls for such things. All we do is collect our monthly rent payments. The net effect is that we have higher monthly cash flow and no unexpected maintenance and repair expenses for the property. This is a wonderful thing.

Comparison of Lease-Option vs. Conventional Rental

3-bedroom, 1-bath house
Market Rent = $500.00, Monthly P.I.T.I. = $375.00

Lease-Option		***Conventional Rental***	
Tenant Payment:	$ 600.00	Tenant Payment:	$ 500.00
(-) Monthly P.I.T.I:	$ 375.00	(-) Monthly P.I.T.I.:	$ 375.00
(-) Repair & Maint:	$ None	(-) Repair & Maint:	$ 40.00
= Net Monthly Cash Flow:	$ 225.00	= Net Monthly Cash Flow:	$ 85.00
Net Annual Cash Flow:	*$2,700.00*	*Net Annual Cash Flow:*	*$1,140.00*

More spendable cash flow with a Lease-Option!

Profit Center 3 – Back-end Option

Finally, we have the option price. The price for which we sell the property is typically 10% to 20% over fair market value. The rationale for this is since we are providing the intermediate financing and bearing the risk for the next few years, we are entitled to capture the appreciation that might come along with it. However, if the tenants make substantial improvements, they receive the benefits of our commitment to cap the price. In effect, they create some "sweat equity."

One of the techniques we use to sell an imperfect or a physically distressed property is by giving a large "repairs and decoration credit." It is far easier for us to give credits on the "back-end", which may or may not be exercised, then to come up with the funds to make repairs to a property ourselves.

Not only do we receive a price higher than market value, but we also leverage this into incentive credits for our tenants to make repairs and improve the property.

As you can see, a lease-option transaction when implemented with some knowledge and creativity, can potentially have three profit centers and provide immense stability within an investor's portfolio. As an investor, the reduction of investment volatility is incredibly important.

Summary

Clearly, I am a proponent of lease-options. They allow my company to create incredible returns for ourselves and out investment partners with minimal overhead. The secret to success of lease-option transactions is not simply the legal instrument, but the tenant's intense desire to buy a home, which allows for fantastic performance within our investment portfolio.

If you're looking for an innovative investment strategy, you should consider lease-options. The first step to successfully implementing lease-options is to not fall into the conventional rental mindset; but keeping an open mind to alternative possibilities.

TurnKey Investing with Lease-Options

Live Events

Matthew Chan & Wes Weaver occasionally speak and make appearances at different educational events within the U.S. and even outside the U.S. They enjoy meeting and networking with other entrepreneurs and investors.

Visit *www.turnkeyinvesting.com* for the latest schedule!

TurnKey Investing with Lease-Options

Onsite Consulting & Training

If you are a Real Estate Agency, Property Managment, or Investment Management firm, and want to implement the TurnKey Investing Lease-Options System within your organization, consider our Onsite Consulting & Training Services.

This elite program is specially designed for corporate organizations.

Onsite Consulting & Training Fees start at $10,000 per day.

Please contact us at *www.turnkeyinvesting.com* for more information!

Ascend Beyond Publishing
www.ascendbeyond.com

Proof of Purchase
The TurnKey Investor's "Subject to" Mortgage Handbook